The War on [illegible] a

Having engaged in an intensified war against corruption for more than four decades since the period of reform and opening up, China is now at a turning point in its anti-corruption agenda. Many believe that building government integrity has been a top-down process in China, and the anti-corruption strategies taken by the current administration seem to have confirmed it. This book challenges the view by analyzing local anti-corruption innovations in recent years and argues for the importance of bottom-up efforts in controlling corruption.

The book attempts to answer the question of whether the rise of local anti-corruption innovations has helped China to pursue anti-corruption reform more effectively and, if so, why. It proceeds to analyze the major patterns of local anti-corruption innovations, the ways in which they have been initiated and implemented, and the factors influencing their success or failure. The book includes more than 400 cases of local innovative anti-corruption reforms in China in recent years.

This book will be a useful reference for those interested in learning more about anti-corruption studies and also contributes to the study of corruption and anti-corruption reform in China by providing solid and fresh evidence of anti-corruption innovation by local governments.

Sunny L. Yang is an Assistant Professor in Department of Public Administration, School of Government, Sun Yat-Sen University. Her research interests mainly focus on corruption and anti-corruption reform, local innovations, and civil service management. She publishes in both Chinese and English in *The China Review*, *Oxford Research Encyclopedia of Politics*, *Fudan Political Science Review*, and so on.

China Policy Series
Series Editor: Zheng Yongnian, Advanced Institute of Global and Contemporary China Studies, Chinese University of Hong Kong (Shenzhen)

61. **Designing Emergency Management**
    China's Post-SARS Experience, 2003-2012
    Wee-Kiat Lim

62. **China's Environmental Foreign Relations**
    Heidi Wang-Kaeding

63. **The Decline of the Western-Centric World and the Emerging New Global Order**
    Contending Views
    Edited by Yun-han Chu and Yongnian Zheng

64. **China's Provinces and the Belt and Road Initiative**
    Dominik Mierzejewski

65. **Women Migrants in Southern China and Taiwan**
    Mobilities, Digital Economies and Emotions
    Beatrice Zani

66. **Great Power Strategies—The United States, China, and Japan**
    Quansheng Zhao

67. **Civilization and the Chinese Body Politic**
    Yongnian Zheng

68. **The War on Corruption in China**
    Local Reform and Innovation
    Sunny L. Yang

For more information about this series, please visit: https://www.routledge.com/China-Policy-Series/book-series/SECPS

The War on Corruption in China

Local Reform and Innovation

Sunny L. Yang

Routledge
Taylor & Francis Group
LONDON AND NEW YORK

Designed cover image: © Getty Images

First published 2023
by Routledge
4 Park Square, Milton Park, Abingdon, Oxon OX14 4RN

and by Routledge
605 Third Avenue, New York, NY 10158

Routledge is an imprint of the Taylor & Francis Group, an informa business

ISBN: 9780367630867 (hbk)
ISBN: 9780367630898 (pbk)
ISBN: 9781003112105 (ebk)

DOI: 10.4324/9781003112105

Typeset in Galliard
by KnowledgeWorks Global Ltd.

Contents

List of Illustrations

Figure

Maps

Tables

List of Acronyms

ACA	Anti-corruption Agency
CCL	Chinese Criminal Law
CPC	Communist Party of China
CPPCC	Chinese People's Political Consultative Conference
CDIC	Central Discipline Inspection Commission
DIC	Discipline Inspection Committee
ICAC	Hong Kong Independent Commission Against Corruption
NDRC	National Development and Reform Commission
NGO	Non-governmental Organization
NSC	National Supervision Commission
RCCK	Revolutionary Committee of the Chinese Kuomintang
SASAC	State-owned Assets Supervision and Administration Commission of the State Council
SOE	State-owned Enterprise

Foreword

Having engaged in an intensified war against corruption for four decades, China is now at a turning point in its anti-corruption reform. Many believe that building government integrity has been a top-down process in China, and the anti-corruption strategies taken by the current administration under Xi Jinping seem to have confirmed this. This book challenges that view by analyzing local anti-corruption innovations in recent years and argues for the importance of bottom-up efforts in controlling corruption. Since the early 2000s, local governments have become more proactive in China's battle against corruption, as demonstrated by numerous local innovations and initiatives. Local anti-corruption innovation has become an important component of and a trend in China's endeavor to tackle corruption.

Understanding local governments' dynamics, patterns, and constraints in making and implementing anti-corruption innovations helps address the puzzling question of how China can pursue anti-corruption reform more effectively. Specifically, this study attempts to analyze local anti-corruption innovations by examining the major patterns in local anti-corruption innovations, how they are initiated and implemented, and what factors have influenced their success or failure.

This study presents 437 local innovative anti-corruption cases from 2013 to 2016 (directly after the 18th National Congress of the Chinese Communist Party), divided into three types: implementation of central anti-corruption policies at local levels; application of new techniques in anti-corruption efforts; and locally initiated anti-corruption methods. While the first two types also serve anti-corruption purposes, this study focuses on the third one, namely the innovative anti-corruption measures developed by local governments. These locally initiated anti-corruption efforts have encountered various difficulties; consequently, some failed while others managed to succeed. Drawing on an "institutional void" analytical framework, this study explores the explanations for success and failure by analyzing local anti-corruption innovations' dilemmas and institutional constraints. It investigates in depth four major local innovation cases in Guangdong: the integrated Office of Integrity in Hengqin, the Qianhai Anti-corruption Bureau, the Integrity Pension Fund in Jiangmen, and the reform of government vehicle management in Shenzhen. This study's findings indicate that although local governments' administrative autonomy is growing, there is no guarantee they can succeed in their attempts to create and implement innovative policies without central blessing, bottom-up support, institutional collaboration, and a legal foundation for proposed innovations.

This study enriches anti-corruption studies by challenging the conventional understanding that anti-corruption reform in China depends on a top-down approach motivated by the central government. It contributes to the study of corruption and anti-corruption reform in China by providing solid and fresh evidence of anti-corruption innovation by local governments. The findings show that the survival and development of local anti-corruption innovations are institutionally constrained, depending on whether they can receive political, organizational, and social support.

Acknowledgments

First and foremost, I would like to express my deepest gratitude to my PhD supervisor, Prof. Gong Ting. She provided continuous support during my PhD study with her patience and immense knowledge. I have been very fortunate to have had her company and motherly care throughout this research. I cannot imagine a better supervisor for my PhD study.

I would also like to thank the members of my thesis committee: Prof. Wang Xiaohu, Dr. Zhu Jiangnan, and Dr. Zhong Yueying, for their insightful comments and critical questions that enlightened me to widen my research.

My sincere thanks also go to my fellow PhD students for the stimulating discussions, the sleepless nights we worked together to meet deadlines, and all the tears and joys we have shared. They are Wang Daan, Ding Tuo, He Chenyang, Zhu Zi, Zhang Yue, Chen Shuo, Xu Jingyuan, and Yuan Lei. In particular, I am grateful to Dr. Xiaohanyu for enlightening me and sharing his experience in doing research. I also want to extend my gratitude to the administrative staff in the Department of Public Policy, especially to Cris, Alvin, and Matt. I also thank my friends outside the academia, Qingqing, Yuewen, and Wu Meng, for supporting me and caring about me, though they are not in Hong Kong.

My research was supported by the Hong Kong University Grants Committee. I am also grateful to *The Chinese University of Hong Kong Press* for granting the copyright of empirical data from the publication: Gong Ting and Sunny L. Yang (2020) Why Do Innovations Succeed or Fail? Local Anti-corruption Reform in China. *The China Review*, 20(4), 69–94. During my fieldwork, I received a lot of help from scholars and government officials. I was fortunate to get help from Prof. Ni Xing, Prof. Li Hui, and interviewees who shared information and views with me.

Last but not least, I would like to thank my parents for their selfless love. This study is dedicated to them.

1 Introduction

Local Anti-Corruption Innovations in China

This chapter is a brief introduction to the study. Section 1.1 presents the definition of the primary terms mentioned in this study and clarifies the research topic's main content. Section 1.2 discusses the context of local anti-corruption innovations. It is followed by Section 1.3, which illustrates the study's research design and indicates its validity. Section 1.4 introduces the main conclusions and implications of this study. Finally, Section 1.5 presents the structure of the book.

1.1 Research Background

The Chinese government has been making efforts in the anti-corruption battleground. Gong (2014) summarized that China's anti-corruption efforts have roughly gone through several stages since 1949: campaign-style enforcement, power-driven anti-corruption, and institutional reform. China largely adopted a top-down approach to fighting corruption in the past, which raised some concerns about its anti-corruption efforts. One concern is the effectiveness of this approach, as it is evident that local conditions vary and that one "size" does not fit all and local governments cannot deal with specific local situations without tailor-made strategies. The other concern is about the sustainability of this approach. With the deepening of the top-down anti-corruption efforts, local officials would adjust their behavior in upper-level government investigations. Thus, the continuity of top-down anti-corruption measures is questionable.

Despite previous top-down anti-corruption enforcement, a new noticeable phenomenon is that local anti-corruption innovations have mushroomed in the last decade. Local governments have shown growing enthusiasm for corruption prevention and made significant efforts at building integrity. I collected 437 cases of local anti-corruption innovations made from 2013 to 2016, covering 29 provinces and taking diverse forms. The number and diversity of these cases are evidence of local enthusiasm for anti-corruption innovations. The phenomenon also challenges the perception that anti-corruption efforts have thus far followed a top-down model. I will further illustrate the cases in Chapter 4.

DOI: 10.4324/9781003112105-1

Though local governments have made significant efforts in anti-corruption innovations, the political environment for the innovations has changed. The 18th National Congress of the CPC marked a turn away from local initiatives back toward a traditional top-down way of combating corruption. A list of corruption cases is evidence of the top-down anti-corruption efforts undertaken since the 18th National Congress. According to the statistics of the Initium Media,[1] among the 205 members of the 18th central committee, 10 have been dismissed from their positions, including the ex-director of the SASAC (State-owned Assets Supervision and Administration Commission of the State Council) in September 2013 and the Municipal Party Committee Secretary of Tianjin in September 2016. Among the 171 alternate members of the Party Committee, 13 have been dismissed from their positions, including the vice secretary of the Sichuan Provincial Party Committee at the end of 2012 and the former executive vice governor of Jiangsu Province in May 2016.

The future of local innovations seems questionable. The following questions should be addressed to understand the past path and further development of China's anti-corruption reform, particularly concerning local innovations: How were local anti-corruption innovations framed and formalized? Will the local-driven anti-corruption innovation become a new trend in China's anti-corruption reform? What is the central government's attitude toward local anti-corruption innovations? Will local enthusiasm last long? Finally, what are the patterns, processes, and dynamics of local anti-corruption innovation in China? This research will try to answer these questions by analyzing four innovative cases in Guangdong Province.

1.1.1 Definition of key terms

Before getting into the details of this research, we must define its key terms—corruption, innovation, local government innovation, and local anti-corruption innovation—to form a logical chain for readers to follow and understand. They also set a clear boundary for what the terms mainly refer to in this study. I borrowed some definitions or explanations from existing research and changed them slightly to fit my research purpose, thereby engaging in a dialogue with the existing literature on innovation, corruption, and anti-corruption practices in China.

1.1.1.1 Corruption

The term "corruption" has been defined in many ways from three points of view: public office, the public interest, and public opinion (Friedrich, 1966: 74; Johnston, 1996: 331; Nye, 1967: 419). The World Bank and most scholars work with a straightforward definition—the abuse of public office for private gain (Tanzi, 1998). This study adopts this definition and views all misconduct committed by those in public positions to advance their personal interests as corruption, since the research object of this study is mainly public officials involved in or affected by innovative cases.

1.1.1.2 Innovation

Generally speaking, policy innovation is a first attempt at implementing a policy (Fagerberg, Mowery, & Nelson, 2005). Previous studies (Boehmke & Witmer, 2004; Heywood, 1965: 107; Mohr, 1969: 112; Rogers, 1983; Thompson, 1965: 2; Walker, 1969; Walker et al., 2002; Zhu, 2014: 119) suggest that "in the field of public administration, innovation is a process of creating or developing projects, services, institutions, or policies that are relatively new to the government ... If a public service innovation is presented in the form of a new policy implemented, we can therefore also call it a policy innovation." Innovation, a key concept in this research, specifically refers to innovative policymaking and implementation.

Innovation is contested. To achieve policy innovation, one has to consider different contexts. Innovations are made for various reasons; some are for better public service provision, and others may be implemented to achieve institutional legitimacy (Walker, 2006). In this study, China's authoritarian regime is the overall background against which to understand innovations by local governments. The fundamental question for innovation research is how innovations occur (Fagerberg et al., 2005). The dynamics of local anti-corruption innovations are the first focus of this study. To help us further understand innovations, the second focus will be on the difficulties and dilemmas innovations may face. The regional differences in making innovations may reflect the unbalanced capability of policy learning across various regions. It would be interesting to explore the dynamic of various innovations and their applicability within and across regions.

1.1.1.3 Local governments' innovation

National-level innovations matter in enhancing the capability of governance. As reviewed by Philip Cooke, Mikel Gomez Uranga, and Goio Etxebarria (1997), the importance of national-level innovation has been mentioned in the research findings of Lundvall (1992), Nelson (1993), and Edquist (1997), especially concerning small-scale countries. National-level innovation "echoes the interesting and important experience of small countries, incapable of investing public research budgets over a wide range of technological areas and possessing relatively few large corporations, therefore having to be selective about areas of innovative strength and well-organized to monitor and absorb valuable innovations from elsewhere" (Cooke & Uranga, 1997: 476). Larger countries "generalize or even abstract from the effects of national political economies in seeking to specify a models of a generic innovation system at the national level" (Cooke & Uranga, 1997: 476). Since it is hard to find a "one size fits all" model, bottom-up innovations are cherished in large countries. According to Borins' analysis of US public sector innovations, a substantial proportion (50%) of public-sector innovation comes from middle-level management and the front lines (Borins, 2002). Public management innovation from the bottom-up has become a subject of considerable academic interest. Innovations could enhance efficiency, effectiveness, and creativity, and successful cases have been presented as role models to follow (Wikhamn, 2011).

Innovation at the local level carries great importance, especially regarding further diffusion. Diffusion means that a policy is applicable in other places, and thus could have greater impact and significance. Innovation diffusion is concerned with the distribution of innovation through a population of potential adopter organizations over time and space (Wolfe, 1994). According to Walker (2006), three major factors determine it: the role of the leader, the benefit to decision-making, and competition among local governments (Walker, 2006: 316).

Local innovation is an important phenomenon in China's reform era. When the decentralization of administrative and economic power has become a focus of reform and the central government has encouraged local policy initiatives, local authorities have made good use of the space for reform and innovation. The central government encourages local experiments at the grassroots level to deepen reforms by providing them with awards and incentives. In 2000, the Central Compilation and Translation Bureau (*zhongyang bianyi ju*/中央編譯局) established the Award for Local Innovations (地方政府創新獎).[2] The bureau rewards successful innovative cases once every two years. Local-level innovations cover most policy areas, including economic development, finance, healthcare, education, and other subtopics. For example, some locally initiated economic policies have grown into models for other areas to learn from, such as the "South Jiangsu model" (蘇南模式) and "Wenzhou model" (溫州模式) in the development of townships, village enterprises, and private enterprises (Chen, 2003). The central government praised these innovative practices at an early stage and they spread to other regions.

However, the central government takes a more prudent attitude toward local anti-corruption innovations than other general innovations (Li, 2015). Li (2015) argued that the underlying reason for the central government to be relatively conservative in endorsing anti-corruption innovations is related to the nature of anti-corruption innovations. Unlike other kinds of innovation that may bring about positive effects, such as resolving social conflicts, innovations in local integrity management may not produce direct output and may even trigger crises in the bureaucratic system. This is because anti-corruption innovations may pursue higher efficiency of public services, rigorous personnel management, and reduction of public expenditure, which could affect individual government officials' interests. Thus, the central government only expresses its approval of anti-corruption innovations that are confined to a particular region. Hence, close observation of anti-corruption innovations at local levels sheds light on corruption and anti-corruption efforts in China's political setting.

1.1.2 Types of local innovations

Local government innovation may be further distinguished into two types based on their relationships with the central government: centrally inspired pilot programs and locally initiated innovations. The former gets approved by the central government beforehand, while the latter does not, which means they both make innovative efforts locally, albeit through different channels: top-down and bottom-up. These two types of innovation epitomize China's policymaking and implementation process.

1.1.2.1 The centrally inspired pilot program

The first type is the centrally inspired pilot program designed by the central government and implemented at local levels. The pilot program involves trying out a policy in a particular area before implementing it at the national level. If the policy experiment turns out to be effective, it will be widely used in other areas. This helps avoid possible risks the political and economic reform would encounter:

> *Local experiments are the hallmark of how China has undertaken all sorts of reforms since the end of the Mao era in the late 1970s. The Chinese approach is less Big Bang and more 'learning-by-doing', an increment list spirit often captured as 'crossing the river by feeling the stones.'*
>
> (Florini, Lai, and Tan, 2012)

The purpose of making policy experiments is to avoid high losses in case the conditions for implementing a policy are not well prepared. In Deng Xiaoping's words, "before we reach a unified national plan, we could start from a region or industry, and gradually open to other parts. The central department should allow and encourage local governments to do the experiments."[3] The top-down pilot programs carry a dual mandate, to consolidate the policy at the local level and to diffuse it to a broader regional area. As summarized by Heilmann, "the point-to-surface (*you dian dao mian*/由點到面) technique gives room to local officials to develop models on their own, while ultimate control over confirming, revising, terminating and spreading model experiments rests with top-level decision makers" (Heilmann, 2013). This is true for anti-corruption practices. In the anti-corruption battleground, the local experiment is a strategy the central government adopts to test the feasibility of a particular policy. For example, Liuyang, Aletai, and Cixi were the first batch of areas where the central government tried out a new integrity measure in 2009–2010, namely, the property declaration of public officials (公務員財產公開). The call for declaration, later on, became a policy practiced in other cities, such as Beijing, Taian, Xi'an, and Pingxiang. The central government only set the general rules for local governments to follow; each city made its own policy, which did not apply to other places and had not yet become a national policy.

1.1.2.2 Locally initiated innovation

Locally initiated innovation goes one step further than the centrally inspired experiment. It refers to those reforms implemented by local governments without initial permission from the central government. Locally initiated innovation aims to make tailor-made policies that better suit the local situation. The "Wenling Model" (溫嶺模式), for example, took the lead in government budget reform by making the first move to a participatory budget, which introduced democratic deliberation in budgeting at the municipal level. Locally initiated innovation is usually carried out with strong local leadership and local funding support. Its purposes are, first, to get routinized locally and, second, to influence central policymaking.

Since the onset of the market reform in the early 1980s, administrative decentralization has been underway within the government. Local governments and enterprises received more decision-making and financial autonomy than in the planned economy era. Some scholars describe this financial decentralization as "fiscal federalism" (Jin, Qian, & Weingast, 2005). Not limited to fiscal decentralization, overall decentralization enhances local governance and gives rise to local experimentation (Bardhan & Mookherjee, 2006). According to Heilmann's study, central policy-makers encourage local officials to try new ways of problem-solving and then feed the local experiences into national policy formulation. This has been pervasive in China's economic transformation (Heilmann, 2008).

A large number of locally-initiated reforms took place even without the permission of upper-level authorities. In the 1990s, local governments frequently took the lead in searching for new governing ways. "Many politically important initiatives, not just the administrative reforms but also initiatives related to transparency, civil society, and even elections, began as local efforts to address local problems without advance permission or even the knowledge of the center" (Florini, Lai, & Tan, 2012: 47).

1.1.2.3 Local anti-corruption innovation

Local governments are also taking more responsibility in the anti-corruption battleground; local anti-corruption innovation is defined as adopting a new policy or measure to combat corruption. It includes both locally initiated innovation and centrally inspired local experiments that aim to enhance government integrity. Local governments have become increasingly important in China's battle against corruption since the 2000s, as seen in the emergence of many local innovations and new measures taken by local governments.

Local integrity management is an important aspect of local governance. I collected 437 cases of local anti-corruption innovations from 2013 to 2016, covering almost all provinces in China, indicating that local government innovation has been a common phenomenon despite the centralization trend since 2013. These innovations include but are not limited to the construction of a culture of clean government, anti-corruption with the help of netizens (internet users), the disclosure of government officials' assets and income, and regular scrutiny of anti-corruption performance. Anti-corruption reform presents a picture of regional disparity, which distinguishes China's current anti-corruption effort from its past.

Scholars have long recognized that anti-corruption and governance are correlated. Kaufman (2005) defined governance as the traditions and institutions by which authority in a country is exercised for the common good. While this is a broader concept than corruption, there is no denying that fighting corruption serves good governance.

1.2 Local Anti-corruption Innovations in China

1.2.1 Context: Adaptation of authoritarian regimes

Policy innovation is a way to adapt to institutional change beforehand. A fruitful discussion has been conducted on the adaptation of authoritarian regimes represented by China. Scholars debate the survival and sustainability of the Chinese Communist Party-State and hold three different views: the optimistic, pessimistic, and middle ground.

Some have a pessimistic view and believe the political system is fragile and beset by systematic economic and ideological crises, and the regime will break down in years rather than decades (Pei, 2006; Shirk, 2007). Another group of scholars takes an optimistic view. They find several significant changes taking place in China's party-state and argue that the Communist Party of China (CPC) will sustain its ruling status: various economic reforms that have spurred various governance reforms leading to a strengthened party-state (Yang, 2006); generational change and leadership turnover of the top leaders of the CPC, and the progressive social policies of the Hu-Wen government—which specifically refers to the then General Secretary, Hu Jintao, and the then Prime Minister, Wen Jiabao (Li, 2012); orderly succession processes in the sense of non-violent power transfer, meritocratic promotions, bureaucratic differentiation, and channels of mass participation and appeal (Nathan, 2003); evolution of a "revolutionary party" into a "ruling party" (Fewsmith, 2003); evolution of the one-party system according to a three-stage typology of transformation, consolidation, and adaptation (Huntington, 1991); a feeling of security from the recruitment of the entrepreneur class into the Party when embedded with the party-state (Dickson, 2000); and unwillingness on the part of private entrepreneurs and the emergent middle class to demand regime change (Tsai, 2006). Based on these analyses, the second group of scholars holds that the CPC can sustain its ruling power in the long run. The third group adopts a middle ground. Shambaugh argued that the CPC is in a simultaneous state of atrophy and adaptation. The adaptation can stabilize, and even reverse, the process of atrophy (Shambaugh, 2008).

Institutional innovations play a role in the problem-formation and solution phases of adaptation. In China, a positive relationship has existed between decentralization and corruption since the economic reform. With growing local autonomy in economic development following the launch of the market economy, local officials have increased opportunities and perhaps incentives to engage in corruption. On the other hand, policy innovations in the anti-corruption field show local governments' vigorous reactions to rampant corruption. In this study, I view innovation as a part of the CPC's adaptation strategy in its political, economic, and social transition since the reform era. In the context of an authoritarian regime, the logic of innovation would be viewed as institutional adaptations ranging from slight technological innovation to structural institutional change, subject to specific local conditions.

1.2.2 Theme: Anti-corruption efforts in local governments

To learn more about studies on China's corruption and anti-corruption efforts, I conducted a review of two bibliographies from the *Routledge Handbook of Corruption in Asia* (edited by Ian Scott and Ting Gong) and the *Oxford Bibliography of Corruption and Anti-corruption in China* (compiled by Sun Yan and Yuan Baishun), respectively. These two bibliographies cover most corruption and anti-corruption studies of China in the past four decades. Based on the review, I find that the number of studies on corruption in China far exceeds the number of works about China's anti-corruption efforts.

Corruption studies cover the causes, features, and consequences of corruption and the relationships between corruption and other factors, such as economic development and governance. Anti-corruption studies discuss such topics as the efficiency of anti-corruption agencies (ACAs), anti-corruption campaigns, and people's perceptions of anti-corruption efforts.

The causes and features of corruption are the main topics in corruption-related studies. Corruption studies have naturally evolved from focusing on corruption to offering more analyses of anti-corruption efforts because the latter should be based on fruitful research into corruption. If we view corruption as a social disease, then policymakers and scholars engaging in anti-corruption studies are social doctors. They have to learn the symptoms of corruption in the first place and then work out appropriate prescriptions to cure it.

This research attempts to increase the empirical data on and theoretical thoughts about anti-corruption studies. Some local corruption and anti-corruption studies have been conducted, for example, the *Routledge Handbook of Corruption in Asia* (2017). As the authors of the *Handbook* pointed out, Asia is home to the largest diversity of corruption and anti-corruption strategies. Quah (2006) classified Asian countries using a matrix of their anti-corruption strategies. He identified their political will (strong vs. weak) and anti-corruption measures (adequate vs. inadequate) to indicate whether it is in a realm of possibility for a particular Asian country to curb corruption. In Quah's analytical framework, China is one of the least likely countries to eliminate corruption, having the least political will and fewest anti-corruption measures.

I believe that the experiences and lessons from China offer people a better understanding of how authoritarian regimes deal with corruption. Taking a close look at some specific cases, we can see the institutional constraints and dynamics facing local governments in making anti-corruption innovations. More information about corruption and anti-corruption studies in China can be found in Chapter 2.

1.2.3 Focus: Local governments

Having been heavily engaged in a war against corruption for several decades, China is now at a turning point in its anti-corruption reform. China has transitioned from a top-down anti-corruption strategy to a more complex stage in the process, with a combination of axial directions and growing local efforts. Although scholars have had productive discussions on central-level anti-corruption practices, they have not given much attention to local governments' role in anti-corruption reform.

Scholars agree that "campaign-style anti-corruption enforcement" is not an effective way to combat corruption and that the current situation requires the government to take more effective measures to control and prevent corruption:

> *Corruption in China has become steadily more "intense" as both the amounts of corrupt monies and the number of senior cadres implicated in corruption have increased dramatically, leading many to view China's "war on corruption" as half-hearted and ineffectual.*
>
> (Wedeman, 2005: 93)

There are several reasons why local governments have to take more responsibility in fighting corruption. First, the failure of top-down anti-corruption strategies over the past four decades has given rise to bottom-up efforts. The decentralization of anti-corruption policymaking and implementation may help improve its effectiveness. As Shah pointed out, "decentralized local governance is conducive to reduced corruption in the long run. This is because localization helps to break the monopoly of power at the national level by bringing decision-making closer to people" (Shah, 2006).

Second, the different forms of corruption between coastal and inland regions determine that corruption must be combated in locally specific ways. For example, the private sector is more developed in coastal areas, providing opportunities for collaboration between government officials and business people, while in China's middle and western inland regions, the main form of corruption is the buying and selling of official positions. Therefore, local governments may set regional priorities and take targeted anti-corruption measures (Gong, 2014).

Third, local governments play essential roles in mobilizing citizens to fight corruption, and local officials may make more appropriate decisions based on local conditions. The public's voice is first heard at local levels as people look for solutions from local governments instead of the central government.

The development of local anti-corruption innovation provokes my interest in the following questions: Does locally initiated anti-corruption enforcement indicate a new stage in China's anti-corruption battle? What are the driving forces behind local governments' anti-corruption innovations? Given the anti-corruption storm led by the central administration after the 18th National Congress of the CPC, which shows the central government's ambition and power in the anti-corruption battleground, will local government innovations be supported in the long run? These questions will be addressed in this study.

Innovations in the public sector have drawn scholarly attention in the past decade. Key factors influencing innovations in local governments include individual motivation for innovation, the exterior environment's influence on the workplace culture, and the challenges presented by innovation. "Motivation speaks to inputs, culture addresses the environment, while the magnitude of challenge addresses risk for the people in an organization" (Glor, 2001: 14). Many current studies focus on the actors in innovative policymaking and how these policies diffuse. Some scholars point out that collaborative governance among different stakeholders contributes to policy innovation. By mobilizing public employees' ideas, knowledge, and entrepreneurship, stakeholders could overcome the problems encountered in executing policy innovations (Sørensen & Waldorff, 2014). A policy-making system requires a dense web of relationships connecting states, companies, civil society organizations, and individuals (Kay & Baker, 2015).

This study will address the following question by analyzing several cases: What conditions make innovations possible and sustainable? This study proposes to reveal the motivation, process, difficulty, and outcome of innovations in the anti-corruption field. I am also interested in discovering why institutions allow such innovations to happen. I made anti-corruption innovations the object of this study because the boundary for integrity management innovation is somehow different from other administrative areas. For example, compared with economic reforms, integrity management touches upon the crucial interests of government officials. As an old Chinese saying states, it is dangerous to ask a tiger for its skin (與虎謀皮). Thus, it is hard to design and carry out anti-corruption innovations.

Under different regimes, there have been diverse channels for new demands to spread upwards from the grassroots level to the state through, for example, relatively peaceful elections or more radical contentious actions. In China, what channels will the central government accept to achieve the same goals as other regimes? How do different actors play their roles in this policy process? How are innovations shaped and become policies that can be implemented locally? Why does the central government react positively or, at least, neutrally to these innovations?

Innovations within the political system have become alternative channels to express the concrete pursuit of combating corruption from the bottom level. To some extent, when the government adopts a new policy, it becomes a successful channel to express bottom-up demands to upgrade anti-corruption measures.

In other words, the upper-level government accepts and tolerates such expressions of interest. This is the first step in an innovation acquiring acceptance from above; the next step is to gain sustainability.

I regard anti-corruption innovation at local levels as a kind of policy innovation. Studies on policy innovations abound (Chen, 2003; Chien, 2007; Naughton, 1994; Nelson & Winter, 1977). Policy innovation involves adopting or creatively exploring a new policy instead of adhering to traditional policies. From this view, anti-corruption innovation matches the features of institutional innovation. While government innovation usually goes through three major phases—initiation, adoption, and implementation—research on implementation is relatively inadequate (Zhao, 2012). According to Zhao's findings, regional economic factors, regional openness, and available resources are the key factors affecting innovations. Even the same local innovation may have different fates in various areas. By comparing several key factors that affect the implementation of an innovation process, this research might also help us better understand regional differences in anti-corruption innovations.

1.2.4 Conceptual framework: Institutional void

I analyze local anti-corruption innovation through the lens of an institutional framework to address the proposed theoretical and practical puzzles. Since an innovative policy has unique characteristics compared to other policy areas, it either reacts to institutional risks or reconstructs the institution (Nay, 2011). The latter raises my research interest and is further discussed in the empirical part of this study.

An institution is generally defined as "a collection of values and rules, largely normative rather than cognitive in the way in which they impact institution members, and the routines that are developed to implement and enforce those values" (March & Olsen, 2005: 9). Most work on institutional change has employed variance theory to follow the changing role of institutions in innovation. The theory covers four perspectives with various purposes. The first perspective is institutional design. It mainly focuses on the purposeful creation or revision of institutions to address conflicts or social injustices. The role of institutions in this perspective is to reflect the pursuit of conscious choices and behavior that society judges to be prudent and reasonable. The second type is institutional adaptation. Here, the role of institutions is to explain how and why organizations conform to forces in the institutional environment. The third perspective, institutional diffusion, examines how and why specific institutions are adopted (selected) and diffused (retained) in a population. Here, institutional theory has borrowed from and extended organizational ecology and evolution. The last is the collective action perspective, which focuses on the process of institutional change in the inter-organizational field; namely, how new institutional arrangements emerge from interactions among interdependent partisan agents.[4]

This study will adopt the first and second perspectives—institutional design and institutional adaptation—to understand innovative policy in anti-corruption practice.

Specifically, I take the institutional void framework to include the innovations' institutional design and institutional adaptation. The institutional void in this research refers to the lack of conditions for a new policy initiative to start and be sustained. It has three aspects: political endorsement, organizational support, and social approval. The institutional void perspective acts in contravention with the previous approaches, such as the political support or local competitiveness perspectives, though they all attempt to enclose the success or failure of innovations. The framework will be further illustrated in Chapter 4.

1.3 Data Collection

Both quantitative and qualitative methods can be applied to explore the success or failure of innovation. In reality, quantitative methods are constrained by data accessibility, and dependent variables are hard to identify and measure using only quantitative methods. For instance, I attempted a quantitative analysis of the local innovations database but found it inappropriate to answer the "how" question: i.e., how could an innovation be initiated and implemented? When we talk about the difficulties local Discipline Inspection Commissions (DICs) face in making an innovation, we may be unable to identify the innovation's actual drawbacks from superficial data. Stakeholder narratives could provide much more information.

I collected data from three sources to get sufficient information on China's local anti-corruption innovations. First, I conducted fieldwork in five cities and focused on four cases for in-depth analysis. Second, I compiled a database of local innovations for 2013–2016 from the official website of the Central Discipline Inspection Commission (CDIC), consisting of 437 local cases about integrity management. Third, I also collected media reports as supplementary information.

Case study

The interviews were conducted in Shanghai, Beijing, and Guangdong Province. Most interviewees were government officials involved in the innovation; others were scholars whose research area was somehow related to corruption and anti-corruption studies. I organized the cases using the proposed theoretical framework, analyzing each in the order of political, organizational, and social voids.

Database of local anti-corruption innovations

As mentioned above, the database self-explains the general picture of local initiatives in making anti-corruption efforts. With 437 cases across different provinces and levels of local governments, the database serves as a fruitful source for me to describe the innovations' major features, patterns, and trends.

Media reports

Another source of information is media reports. Since the interviewees were somehow related to or affected by the innovations, they may have blurred or concealed some information; thus, using only their narratives was not convincing. Furthermore, as the triangulation principle suggests (Jick, 1979), alternative information sources must be found and combined to gain a complete picture of a phenomenon. Thus, I searched media reports written during the innovations or as follow-up reports for supplementary material. The reports usually provided background information on the innovations, explained the related rules, and combined historical changes. It was interesting to put all this information together and see how the innovations had changed from the beginning.

The coding format (e.g., LAI-2014-12) used in this study implies three layers of information. "LAI" represents the research subject "local anti-corruption innovations," followed by the year the interview was conducted ("2014"). The final number ("12") indicates the 12th interview. For more detailed information, see the attached interview list.

1.4 Major Findings and Implications

1.4.1 Major findings

This study makes three major points based on the review of the overall situation of local anti-corruption innovations and case studies. First, local anti-corruption innovations have become a common phenomenon. They have contributed to the accumulation of local experiences, and some have even expanded to other localities. Second, any local anti-corruption innovation is no easy task and often cannot be sustained. Successful innovation requires institutional support or, more specifically, political endorsement, organizational support, and social approval. Third, anti-corruption innovations are unique compared to other local innovations, carrying more political meanings and catching more social attention.

1.4.2 Implications of the study

Corruption and anti-corruption efforts have now become a daily public topic of discussion in China and local anti-corruption innovations are at the forefront of social opinions. This study provides a theoretical perspective to view the anti-corruption innovations instead of merely attributing anti-corruption efforts to power struggles. Theoretically, this study explains why some local anti-corruption innovations could succeed while others could not, from the institutional void perspective.

This research also has practical implications for local practitioners of anti-corruption innovations. For example, the practitioners should be aware of what kind of support they need when preparing for innovation instead of turning a blind eye to social reflections, as shown in the Jiangmen Case at the beginning of the innovation case section. The lessons help local governments build a possible pathway to make successful innovations or even achieve policy diffusion in a broader area.

The study also provides a possible blueprint for the future trend of local anti-corruption innovations. The future of innovations is a mixed picture as a top-down approach to fighting corruption seems to have returned since the 18th National Congress. Having initiatives from local levels does not necessarily mean a bottom-up approach. There is a long way to go to achieve the real bottom-up effect, i.e., to get the public involved in anti-corruption work and, ideally, make the public's voice heard in anti-corruption policymaking and implementation. Thus, I view the current period as a transition from a top-down to a bottom-up approach. Local governments are the linkage between the central government and the public and play a crucial role in making such transition possible.

Recently, the central government set up a new anti-corruption institution, the National Supervision Commission (NSC), once as a pilot program in Beijing, Zhejiang, and Shanxi Provinces now spread to the national level. It seems that innovations are, once again, mostly initiated by the central government with little local input. This study presents the ups and downs of local anti-corruption innovations and their future, which remains a mystery as it is too early to know their effects.

1.5 Structure of the Book

This study is composed of eight chapters, organized as follows:

Chapter 1 is the introduction, which provides the background information about corruption and anti-corruption narratives of China since 1949. It first clarifies the definitions of the major terms in this study and justifies why I chose to study local governments' anti-corruption efforts. Following that, I present the study's plan and introduce its arrangement.

Chapter 2 is a literature review of the studies, both at home and abroad, on anti-corruption practices and local governments' anti-corruption innovations in China. The subtopics include general questions, such as the causes and characteristics of corruption; how to combat corruption from institutional, economic, and organizational perspectives; the global trend of building a local integrity system; and local governments' growing anti-corruption reform efforts in China. The extant studies mainly discuss the motivations of local governments in conducting anti-corruption innovations, but do not investigate the dilemmas of local innovation. This research focuses on the underlying factors impeding the sustainability of local innovations and illustrates these obstacles using case studies. A discussion of the research questions—concerning the patterns, dilemmas, and institutional constraints of local governments' anti-corruption innovation—follows.

Chapter 3 is a historical overview and reviews the history of anti-corruption studies in China. Looking back on 40 or more years of anti-corruption practice in China, I reveal the changing foci and features of anti-corruption strategies. I examine the political and economic backgrounds affecting forms of corruption and corresponding anti-corruption strategies through the evolving anti-corruption regulations from 1979 until the present.

Chapter 4 outlines 437 cases of local integrity management innovations to change perceptions of China's corruption-fighting strategies in recent years by presenting general information on how local governments achieve their anti-corruption innovations efforts. The analytical framework of this study follows, i.e., the institutional void and institutional foundation of anti-corruption innovations, together with the theory and methods used to elaborate on China's innovative anti-corruption policymaking and implementation. I adopt an institutional void framework to make the general idea of "institutional foundation" feasible and distinct enough for readers to understand. "Institutional void" in this research refers to the lack of political, organizational, and social foundations for a new policy initiative.

Chapters 5–7 are empirical chapters that illustrate and analyze four cases that could represent anti-corruption efforts initiated by local governments in Guangdong Province.

Chapter 5 presents Jiangmen City's attempt to make an innovative policy, the Integrity Pension Fund, to ensure integrity by government officials through economic incentives. Jiangmen was the first municipal government to try such a policy. This case failed because of harsh social criticism. Political support, while initially sufficient, withered afterwards due to social restrictions. Public opinion is that it is unnecessary to encourage public servants to keep clean by increasing their salaries. Though the organizational cooperation went well, despite harsh public criticism, the innovation was ultimately terminated by the provincial DIC.

Chapter 6 introduces the Integrity Management Office of Hengqin and the Anti-corruption Bureau of Qianhai, both of which attempted structural changes to anti-corruption agencies, i.e., integrating several ACAs into one body. While alike in their underlying intentions, these two innovations differed in strategy. Hengqin and Qianhai have similar geographic locations and political intentions but took different approaches to similar institutional changes to their ACAs. The two cases had different fates due to their diverse organizational structures, since the innovation was determined by how they dealt with organizational disputes.

Chapter 7 presents the reform of government vehicles in Shenzhen, which aimed to reduce the abuse of public vehicles by cutting down the number of government vehicles and providing subsidies to government officials affected by the reform. Being one of the first cities to make innovations on reform of government vehicles, Shenzhen eventually achieved its innovation goal. Despite encountering difficulties during the policy design and implementation process, it overcame the challenges through strong political will, organizational negotiation, and the public's understanding.

I analyze the four cases through an institutional void framework, finding that three pillars must exist for innovation to emerge and last: political, organizational, and societal support. Among these three, political support weighs the most and is vital to innovation; however, that does not mean that the other two factors are unimportant.

Chapter 8 concludes this book by presenting its main findings and identifying future research directions for and discussions on this topic. This study shows the overall situation of local efforts in making anti-corruption innovations. Based on the historical overview and literature review, I summarize the patterns of innovations and how they could achieve success. Future studies could further explore the effectiveness of innovations, the current experiment on the reform of ACAs, and the future of local innovations in a given political setting.

Notes

1 Su Xinqi, The succession of top leaders of the CPC after the 18th National Congress, the Initium Media, Accessed on October 24, 2016, https://theinitium.com/article/20161024-mainland-plenary-6/.

2 Yu Keping, the main organizer of the Award of Local Innovations, once revealed that this award was intended to back up the local governments' courage in taking risks for innovations and to show appreciation for their efforts in advancing public welfare (Yu, 2010). The purpose of this award is also to identify cases of innovation in institutional reform and the provision of public services at local levels, which might apply to other areas.

3 Excerpts from talks given in Wuchang, Shenzhen, Zhuhai, and Shanghai, January 18–February 21, 1992, *Selected Works of Deng Xiaoping*, volume 3.

4 The *Handbook of organizational change and innovation*. New York: Oxford University Press, 2004: P262.

2 Rethinking Approaches to Study

Anti-Corruption in Post-Reform China

In this chapter, I discuss the literature on corruption and anti-corruption reform in China since reform and opening up, according to four main topics: three approaches to corruption and anti-corruption studies in post-reform China; studies on the extent of corruption and evaluation of anti-corruption effectiveness during this time; recent studies on local governments' integrity both in and outside China; and the practice of local innovations in integrity management in China. I review these four topics because the features of corruption and the effectiveness of anti-corruption strategies covered by the first two topics have contributed to the transition from the traditional top-down anti-corruption strategy to a relatively bottom-up one. The literature on the third and fourth topics on the local integrity system is reviewed to answer the research question of how to achieve successful local anti-corruption innovations in China. A theoretical gap exists in the mainstream literature, as limited scholarly attention has been given to local anti-corruption reforms and innovations, especially in China. The literature review also provides background information for my case studies.

By reviewing the extant literature, this study goes one step further and contributes to the general literature on corruption and innovation studies. In the following sections, it will be made clear that local anti-corruption innovations are different in China than outside of China due to different political backgrounds.

2.1 Three Approaches to Corruption Studies in Post-reform China

As a social phenomenon, corruption has a profound effect on regional stability and development. Corruption has been widely recognized to haunt society by damaging social justice, destroying people's faith and trust in the government, and sometimes hampering economic growth.[1] As a result, it has attracted the attention of scholars and practitioners. In studying corruption in China, scholars tend to focus on the causes, characteristics, and forms of corruption (Gong, 1994; Lu, 2000; Sun, 2005). Most studies take the institutional, economic, and

DOI: 10.4324/9781003112105-2

organizational approaches to analyze the causes of corruption and strategies to fight it in China (Birney, 2014; Gong, 2006; Wedeman, 2005).

The factors that lead to corruption in post-reform China have long been of research interest in corruption studies. One group of scholars holds that institutions are responsible for corruption (Fan, Lin, & Treisman, 2009; Gong, 1993). Institutional factors, such as loopholes in the judicial system, an administrative monopoly, and informal behaviors and institutions contribute to corruption. Some scholars attribute corruption to economic reform and enclose the relationship between economic reform and the changing features of corruption (Ko & Weng, 2012; Quade, 2007; Sun, 2005). Another group of authors notes that organizational factors, such as inadequate cadre management and the lack of modernization of the CPC organization, give rise to corruption (Lu, 2000; Zhou, 2009). Scholars have paid attention to regional disparities in the causes of corruption. For example, the resource curse theory has been applied to explain why corruption so often occurs in resource-rich areas (Zhan, 2011). Dong and Torgler (2013: 152) found a much lower occurrence of corruption in regions with more anti-corruption efforts, a history of British rule, greater openness, more access to media, and relatively higher government employee wages. Conversely, social heterogeneity, regulation, resource abundance, and state-owned enterprises (SOEs) substantially breed regional corruption. In the following part, I discuss the institutional, economic, and bureaucratic approaches to illustrate their effect on bringing about corruption. The corresponding solutions proposed by these approaches are discussed after each approach.

2.1.1 *Institutional approach*

First, many scholars believe institutions are the root cause of corruption in China, affecting corruption through policy. From this approach, scholars attribute corruption in China to policy failure outcomes. By analyzing China's general, organizational, and anti-corruption policies and their relationships with corrupt activities from 1949 to 1992, Gong (1993: 311) concluded that corruption from 1949 may have resulted from the unintended consequences of some intended reform policies. These policies, while aimed at transforming China's socioeconomic structures, inadvertently created political and economic conditions favorable to corruption. Based on Rothstein's (2011: 234) observation of corruption in Sweden, he held that corruption is a result of institutions that, as a system, force people to imitate corrupt behaviors because "ordinary people usually condemn corruption as morally wrong and put the blame on 'the system' for forcing them to take part in corruption, thus understanding that they are in a 'social trap' like situation." Guo (2007) attributed corruption to the availability of corruption opportunities, strong motivations, and low institutional constraints. He suggested that the spread of corruption results from institutional change that lags behind economic transition, noting that corruption may occur in unstable political-economic environments that emerge in transitional periods after economic reforms. As Johnston and Hao (1995: 82) pointed out, "[t]he corruption-reform connection is complex. The surge of corruption in China is a consequence not only of market reforms, but also of the politico-economic order that preceded them. That system was built on revolutionary ideology, a charismatic leader, and party-state dominance." Fan et al. (2009) suggested that the decentralization process in China's reform era has contributed to increased corruption, as rapid transition makes it difficult for officials to be self-disciplined. In the decentralization process, large numbers of government and administrative tiers/officials have been suspected of bribery or obtaining illegal economic shares (Fan et al., 2009).

By reflecting on the root causes of corruption, the first possible solution is to treat institutions as a whole and consider systematic and comprehensive reform rather than a single measurement taken directly to fight corruption. Rothstein (2007) pointed out that it might be better to fight corruption by changing political and social institutions instead of dealing with particular institutions or policies one by one. He argued, "[W]hat is needed to establish a new equilibrium of social and economic exchange is a 'big-bang'" (Rothstein, 2007: 3). From the institutional approach, the only solution to contemporary China's growing and severe corruption problem is to improve political and economic institutions to eliminate corruption-inducing loopholes effectively.

2.1.2 Economic approach

Although some scholars do not agree with the institutional analysis and assert that corruption has other causes rooted in China's economic transition. This economic approach considers corruption a byproduct of the growing economy and argues that the features and modes of corruption have evolved with the marketization of China's economy in recent decades. Thus, the government must identify changing market conditions and emerging corruption features to find appropriate anti-corruption measures. Quade (2007) contended that anti-corruption action is an outcome of economic development, finding a correlation between economic austerity rounds and anti-corruption practices by analyzing empirical data from 1981–1997. According to Ko and Weng (2012), China has experienced significant economic and administrative evolution during its economic reform. As the causes of corruption have changed with this evolution, structural changes have taken place within the corruption itself, making it differ from that seen at the beginning of the market reform. For example, the government's role in the market was overwhelming in the 1990s, as market competition was weak and SOEs enjoyed monopolistic power. Since the market reform and expansion of the state's power to intervene in the economy (represented by widespread collaboration among political and economic powers), corruption activities related to economic behaviors have been observed more frequently than ever. Sun (2005) attributed rampant corruption to economic factors, observing a reform paradox featuring high corruption and rampant economic growth.

The state's governance ability lags behind the market transition, thus giving government officials more rent-seeking opportunities.

For those who believe the marketization process gives rise to new forms and high frequencies of corruption, the solution is to improve the market system and encourage economic competition. As Cheng (2000) pointed out, complex relationships exist among organizational streamlining, economic restructuring, and anti-corruption work. However, the market-oriented approach is challenged because corruption problems exist in countries or regions with mature market systems, such as Taiwan and South Korea. The advancement of economic institutions alone cannot be the overall solution to corruption.

2.1.3 Bureaucratic approach

Another group of scholars holds a bureaucratic approach. From this approach, the bureaucratic system is taken as a whole, with the behavior of local governments is interpreted as stemming from bureaucratic organizations. The key is understanding local governments' informal or improvised strategies to carry out bureaucratic tasks. Lu (2000) considered organizational factors of corruption, aside from the changing political economy, especially during the transition from state socialism to a market economy. In Wedeman's words, "Lu's core thesis is that the CPC failed to make the transition from a revolutionary organization to a routinized, rationalized, and bureaucratized institution in which state agents are subject to rule by law and regulation, rather than rule by politics" (Wedeman, 2002: 303). This problem existed before the economic reform, did not improve in the economic transition period, and helps explain the changing patterns of corruption in China after the reform policy was launched. However, without the modernization of the CPC organization, this situation cannot be changed (Lu, 2000). Zhou contended that three organizational paradoxes—uniformity in policymaking and flexibility in implementation; incentive intensity and goal displacement; and bureaucratic impersonality and personalization of administrative ties—provide legitimate bases for collusion among local governments (Zhou, 2009).

For scholars who hold that organizational factors determine corrupt behavior, the solution is to improve the bureaucratic system, especially the cadre management system. Some scholars argue that the CPC's cadre management system has loopholes that help cover up corrupt behaviors and make it difficult to combat corruption. The "rule of mandates," i.e., "China's system of decentralized authoritarian rule" (Birney, 2014: 55), protects officials and is why China encounters difficulty in combating corruption. Under the "rule of mandates," the regime holds its officials accountable for relative, not fixed, standards (Birney, 2014), leaving them room to engage in corruption. The bureaucratic approach provides an alternative way to understand the difficulty of carrying out anti-corruption work at the organizational level, because local governments are subject to their organizational interests. However, this approach alone does not lead to feasible solutions to prevent corruption permitted for bureaucratic reasons.

2.2 Studies on Rampant Corruption and Anti-corruption Effectiveness

2.2.1 Corruption in post-reform China

This section reviews the literature on the degree of corruption in post-reform China. The consensus is that corruption became rampant during the reform era.

Based on Lu (1999: 355), "[N]ew forms of corruption have thus emerged. Since the mid-1980s, a new phenomenon in the growing array of corruption has grown out of control—'organizational rent-seeking' or irregular and illicit behaviors by various state agencies with monopoly power to enrich their units." Though the Chinese government launched inspection regulations to control corruption, the problem has only worsened. Gong (2002) focused on the phenomenon of collective corruption, finding that the relationship between power and wealth draws ever closer and that the utility of political power acts as a means to acquire assets has been more obvious since the 1990s. Society has not yet reached a consensus that corruption is unacceptable and corruption accompanies people's daily life. Unsurprisingly, the introduction of new and a greater number of market mechanisms has led to serious colluding corruption efforts. Wedeman (2004) argued that, during the 1990s, corruption underwent a qualitative change, as high-level, high-stakes corruption increased more rapidly than other forms of official malfeasance. He drew this conclusion from data gathered by three major anti-corruption agencies in China: the CPC's Discipline Inspection Commission, the state supervision, and the procuratorate. By analyzing 594 major corruption cases, Guo (2008) found that the extent of corruption corresponds with the stage of economic transition.

Through a quick review of corruption and anti-corruption studies, we find that scholars and practitioners have agreed on the rampant corruption in post-reform China and thus the importance of anti-corruption effectiveness.

2.2.2 China's anti-corruption efforts

Determining the effectiveness of anti-corruption reforms means evaluating if China has taken appropriate strategies to fight corruption at different stages. Clearly, a top-down anti-corruption strategy is not enough. This section focuses mainly on how anti-corruption effectiveness is measured in China. The existing studies on Chinese anti-corruption efforts include research on anti-corruption agencies (in the Chinese context, mainly the CDIC and DICs) and their effectiveness. Many studies focus on the effectiveness of a frequently observed Chinese style of anti-corruption: campaign-style enforcement. In contrast to those who have discussed the top-down manner of anti-corruption efforts, I discuss the existing bottom-up attempts (i.e., the local anti-corruption innovations), as only a few scholars have attempted to answer the question of how to make local anti-corruption efforts effective and successful.

The literature on China's anti-corruption efforts has addressed China's efforts to fight corruption, specifically, how the Chinese government combats corruption. One consensus is that anti-corruption agencies (ACAs) have played a crucial role in the fight against corruption (Choi, 2009; Meagher, 2005; De Sousa, 2010). "Following the perceived failure of conventional law enforcement bodies (police, courts, attorney-general offices, etc.), ACAs are often regarded by governments, donors, and international governmental organizations (IGOs) as the ultimate institutional response to corruption, an important piece of the national institutional architecture" (Sousa, 2010: 6). This wave of studies focusing on local anti-corruption efforts has led to a branch in corruption study globally—the evaluation of the effectiveness of ACAs (Meagher, 2002). In China's case, ACAs refer to central and local Discipline Inspection and Supervision Commissions. Guo examined four dimensions of the then CDIC's institutional transition during the reform era: its authority, independence, integrity, and professionalism. Authority means the CDIC's political power to carry out its responsibilities and is influenced by the level of support it receives from its power source, the highest leadership and legislature. Independence refers to whether the CDIC's decisions and investigations are free from intervention by political parties, interest groups, or individuals and whether its finances are sufficient and independent. Integrity and professionalism measure the levels of integrity and professionalism of the CDIC's staff, especially its main leaders. The conclusion is that, although the CDIC has gone through a dramatic change by obtaining relatively more authority, independence, integrity, and professionalism than before, the efficacy of its work remains unsatisfactory (Guo, 2012).

2.2.3 The campaign-style anti-corruption strategy

To analyze the effectiveness of China's anti-corruption efforts, scholars contribute their understanding from various angles in addition to specifically researching DICs. Some scholars believe that how governments choose to fight corruption determines the effectiveness of anti-corruption reforms. Manion (2004) conceptualized China's anti-corruption strategy in past decades as "campaign-style enforcement," which emphasizes political factors while ignoring the standardization of laws and regulations. She further illustrated this term as short bursts of intensive enforcement to produce anti-corruption results. Each campaign featured the government "encouraging ordinary Chinese to report corruption and urging corrupt officials to confess their crimes, and new demands by top generalist leaders on local Party agencies to greatly increase the role of the criminal justice system in anti-corruption enforcement" (Manion, 2004: 91). Manion revealed two problems campaign-style enforcement has brought about: increased official rhetoric about "punishment according to the law" and increased pressures on procuratorial resources (Manion, 2004: 92). Wedeman contended that "campaign-style enforcement may have actually contributed to the 'intensification' of corruption" (Wedeman, 2005: 93). Li agreed with Manion's idea. Based on what previous authors pointed out, he further examined the limitation of campaign-style enforcement, finding it does nothing to remove either the patrimonial patron-client network or the client-list patron-client network; it usually lags behind corruption activities and thus does not help prevent corruption (Li, 2010).

Other scholars have applied this term to the analysis of anti-corruption efforts in the early reform period of China (Gong, 2011; Li, 2001; Quade, 2007; Wedeman, 2005). Li (2001), based on data collected from a survey conducted in six provinces at the end of 1997 and early 1998, offered the interesting finding that some peasants would like to see Mao-style anti-corruption campaigns in rural China, despite their negative side effects. Popular support for mass mobilization can contribute to rural instability as Chinese farmers become increasingly impatient with the regime's failure to control corruption. This finding indicates that the adoption of campaign-style enforcement in anti-corruption activities negatively impacts people's belief in the rule of law, especially at the grassroots level. Quade (2007) examined the timing of anti-corruption campaigns by analyzing available data from 1981 to 1997. Four major anti-corruption campaigns were implemented (in 1982, 1986, 1989, and 1993), each coinciding with the end of an inflationary peak and the beginning of a macroeconomic austerity period. Quade established a causal link between anti-corruption campaigns and economic austerity rounds and proposed that anti-corruption campaigns have been used primarily to combat economic overheating rather than corruption. During the reform era, anti-corruption enforcement campaigns mainly served as a viable economic adjustment mechanism. Wedeman (2005) analyzed the efficacy of China's campaign-style anti-corruption strategy using a combination of formal modeling and empirical data. His analysis suggested that although this strategy may succeed in keeping corruption "under control", it is more likely to deter low-level corruption than high-level, high-stakes corruption and may encourage bribe-size inflation. He further concluded that campaign-style enforcement may have intensified corruption.

Gong (2011) found that China changed its strategy from campaign-style enforcement to institutionalizing integrity management because of previous unsuccessful attempts at controlling corruption. She defined this change as an "institutional turn" of the Chinese government, characterized by rule-guided integrity building and manifesting itself in the growth of various local integrity initiatives (Gong, 2011: 671). The recent anti-corruption practice under Xi Jinping's leadership is considered a continuation of campaign-style enforcement, although its nature and consensus may differ (Mulvenon, 2013).

Campaign-style enforcement in anti-corruption efforts is certainly not recommended by scholars because of its side effects, including but not limited to damaging the value of the rule of law, intensifying corruption (as a result of ruining law enforcement), and blocking the development of an institutionalized anti-corruption system.

The views mentioned above can be summarized as follows: campaign-style anti-corruption enforcement, China's political decentralization, loopholes in the cadre management system, and the changing forms of corruption under political and economic conditions are the main factors contributing to the failure of China's past anti-corruption reforms. Scholars (Manion, 2004; Ren, 2013; Wedeman, 2005) have attempted to reveal why China's anti-corruption efforts have been ineffective in the past four decades, but have inadequately studied or underemphasized the role of local governments in the anti-corruption drive.

2.3 A New Trend: the Combination of Top-down and Bottom-up Efforts

The centrally oriented anti-corruption strategy has not met public expectations in recent decades, in part because the central government has not fully accepted the concept of public engagement in corruption control. Therefore, anti-corruption efforts may rely on a combination of top-down and bottom-up approaches. Local efforts in anti-corruption innovations are growing in importance. The performance of local ACAs should be assessed and explained in the context of growing local challenges; they cannot exhibit anti-corruption effectiveness based on higher authorities' pressure. Scholars have found that DICs have started to seek a relatively sustainable path to combat corruption. Gong pointed to "an 'institutional turn' in integrity management in China" (Gong, 2011), characterized by rule-guided integrity-building at the local levels and manifesting itself in the growth of various local integrity initiatives. Shah (2006) suggested that local efforts are important in the overall fight against corruption. Localization helps to break the monopoly of power at the national level by bringing decision-making closer to people. Localization strengthens government accountability to citizens by involving citizens in monitoring government performance and demanding corrective actions. Localization as a means to make government responsive and accountable to people can help reduce corruption and improve service delivery. Efforts to improve service delivery usually force the authorities to address corruption and its causes (Shah, 2006).

2.3.1 Local anti-corruption efforts matter

The national-level integrity system has long been examined by anti-corruption researchers and research teams like Transparency International (TI) and the World Bank (Gurgur & Shah, 2002; Hodess & Wolkers, 2004; Shah, 2006). TI has presented the extent of corruption at the national level using the corruption perception index (CPI) each year since 1995. However, no local-level corruption index has yet been developed, meaning issues like the performance of provincial and municipal integrity systems have received less attention. According to Anechiarico (2009: 80), "[L]ocal government has long been fertile ground for the discovery of fraud, waste and abuse in the public sector."

Some scholars, although not many, have shed light on local governments' anti-corruption efforts (Bedock, 2013; United Nations Development Programme, 2005). Their research covers such topics as the significance of local anti-corruption efforts, how institutions at local levels work together to achieve better anti-corruption effectiveness, the role of local anti-corruption agencies in implementing anti-corruption policies, and how to evaluate the success of a local integrity system. The research findings provide a broad view of local anti-corruption efforts worldwide and help practitioners and theorists identify the experiences and lessons Chinese local governments might learn.

Huberts and colleagues' research on world cities' efforts in fighting corruption and safeguarding integrity identified seven successful "local integrity systems" (Huberts & Six, 2012: 151), including Hong Kong, Sydney, New York City, and London (Huberts, Anechiarico, & Six, 2008), that set good examples for integrity building at the sub-national level. Their research illustrates these local integrity systems' history, supportive conditions, and institutional strengths. Supported by the United Nations Development Programme, the authors focus on organizational cooperation and coherence to combat corruption; "One crucial element of an anti-corruption strategy is to decide on the institutional models for fighting corruption and on the policies and capacity development efforts that will allow these institutions to effectively play their role" (United Nations Development Programme, 2005: 10).[2]

The characteristic of an "integrity system" approach is that it outlines elements and conditions that are important for the integrity of governance. A checklist of policies, institutions, and conditions has to be offered by ACAs and used to describe, analyze, and evaluate what a government has in place. When the approach is applied at the local or city level, the elements must be transformed to reflect that level of government and society (Huberts et al., 2008: 10). The authors examined the "local integrity system" and found several irreplaceable benefits of local-level anti-corruption policies compared with national ones. Local policies are closer to the public and may have a more direct impact on local lives than those at the central level. "[I]t should be acknowledged that people form opinions about government, decide on their level of political participation, and calculate their social capital in terms of what is happening to them and their neighbors in their cities and towns of residence. In essence, the nature and potential of governance in a society is to a large extent determined by where we live" (Huberts et al., 2008: 3). As Anechiarico observed, local ACAs advance inspection, oversight, and approaches to evaluating corruption control that have not been detected in studies on national ACAs (Anechiarico, 2009: 81).

The authors identified several risks for local integrity systems, including that "the different institutions do not cooperate and coordinate their endeavors which might be harmful for the reputation and performance of the system" (Huberts et al., 2008: 12). Here, a critical question is how the efficacy of local ACAs is evaluated. Choi (2009), borrowing the logic of the economics of enforcement, provided an overall anti-corruption effectiveness indicator (AEI) that measures the efficacy of local anti-corruption enforcement. The indicator is constructed as follows: AEI=pd *pa *pp *pc *Penalty, where "pd is the probability of detection, pa is the probability of arrest of given detection, pp is the probability of prosecution given arrest, pc is the probability of conviction given prosecution, and Penalty is the amount of money imposed on offenders. A higher AEI value indicates an effective anti-corruption agency" (Choi, 2009: 202). The indicator combines the probability of detection, arrest of given detection, prosecution, and the amount of money imposed on offenders to measure overall anti-corruption effectiveness. The elements in this explanation can be borrowed to test the local anti-corruption performance.

2.3.2 Evolution of China's local anti-corruption efforts

"Corruption control is most effective when the central public integrity agency is part of both a local anti-corruption network and a local public management network" (Anechiarico, 2009: 79). However, local anti-corruption efforts in China are understudied. In reality, as mentioned in the last chapter, local innovations have flourished in the past few years, manifesting in various initiatives and experiments; some have even caught the attention of the central authorities.

Scholarly attention on this topic in China is limited compared with other regions worldwide. In the reform era, local governments face the administrative paradox, i.e., the "double identity" refined by Gong (2006: 86), which makes them unable to act properly in the central-local relationship. "Double identity" specifically refers to the inner contradictions faced by local governments: they gain both broad discretionary power from the central authorities and immediate economic benefits from managing the local economy; this situation gives rise to corruption at the local level (Gong, 2006). This "double identity" of local governments makes fighting corruption difficult. Examining the role played by local governments in China's anti-corruption efforts under the background of double identity is an exciting topic.

2.4 Role of Local Innovations in China's Anti-corruption Reform

Research on local innovation in China has boomed since the early 2000s, with the growing influence of the "Award for Local Government Innovations" mentioned in the Introduction (Zhu, 2014). The term "experimentation under hierarchy" accurately illustrates the phenomenon that the CPC tries out policies at local levels (Tsai & Dean, 2014). The core of this strategy is to find appropriate policies at a local level in accordance with its actual conditions (*yin di zhi yi/* 因地制宜). Unlike requests for experiments from the top level, local innovations tend to be self-driven and original. Local innovations involve high political risks. In detail, the first risk is to break existing laws as some innovations have to do so to achieve effectiveness. The second risk is that they may be easily understood due to their novelty and may even receive public criticism. Local innovations are mostly led by local cadres and elites and have insufficient public participation. The sustainability of local innovations highly depends on the support from upper-level governments. As long as local governments chose to make innovative policies, risks would go along with them.

2.4.1 Motivations for local anti-corruption innovations

Several scholars have focused on the role of the central government and argued that the central government takes the lead in China's anti-corruption reform (Chen, 2003; Feng, 2011; Zhuang, 2014). Although some scholars have noticed China's bottom-up anti-corruption practices (Gong, 2011; Shah, 2006), studies of local governments' efforts at curbing corruption are inadequate and even less attention has been paid to what motivates local anti-corruption innovations.

Among the limited research on this specific topic, Wang (2009) summarized three motivations for local governments' anti-corruption innovations and practices. First, local governments are pressured by the central level to be innovative. Second, local governments consider that anti-corruption measures may create a better environment for economic development. Third, a cleaner government helps build a better government image for local residents. Yu (2013) collected data from 31 provinces and found that obtaining fiscal resources is local governments' main consideration when launching anti-corruption innovations. Local authorities' developmental rationale, decentralization, power fragmentation, and lack of social accountability are the key reasons for the decline in local financial expenditures on anti-corruption efforts. These factors work together and lead to a decrease in fiscal resources at the local level. Thus, recovering or stopping financial losses caused by corruption is a motivation for local governments. One achievement of anti-corruption work is to reclaim state property from corrupt officials through judicial rulings. Another is cadres' rational choice under the "tournament system" (Zhou, 2009). Local anti-corruption efforts are commonly assessed based on local cadres' performance. The central or higher-level governments organize competitions wherein local governments are evaluated based on local growth, economic performance, policy innovation, and social stability. Local governments, as participants, must meet the goals set by higher authorities. The stimulation mechanisms include, for example, policy advantage and cadre promotion. Zhou (2009) agreed with the analysis and defined the phenomenon as a "promotion tournament" which describes the Chinese mode of cadre promotion.

As a whole, whether local governments are interested in anti-corruption innovation is a disputed issue among scholars. Some scholars believe that local governments in China are struggling to fulfill the tasks assigned by higher authorities, leaving them unlikely to make innovations (Zhou, 2009). Others consider that local governments lack the incentive to innovate because doing so has political risks (Persson, Rothstein, & Teorell, 2013). Scholars suggest that policy innovations can help local governments attract attention and obtain more resources from higher-level authorities. Furthermore, they believe local governments should not lose anything by trying innovative measures. If innovations work out, local governments will benefit; otherwise, local leaders will not be punished anyway (Zhou, 2007).

2.4.2 Regional disparity of local anti-corruption efforts in China

Based on the limited studies on local anti-corruption innovations so far, the effectiveness remains questionable. Wu and Zhu (2011) examined the relationship between corruption and county income levels by conducting a quantitative analysis of 36 counties with data gathered from the China County Statistical Yearbook 2004 and Chinese Audit Yearbook 2003–2004 and found that corruption was negatively correlated with local economic performance. In their view, local governments' anti-corruption endeavors significantly increase local income levels, which is an underlying motivation for local governments to combat corruption. In many localities, anti-corruption innovations do not last long after the person in charge is transferred to a different post unless supported by the citizens, local authorities, and the central government. Three main reasons account for short-lived anti-corruption innovations. First, most innovations challenge existing practices and bring about policy uncertainty. Second, innovations usually provoke conflict among local departments that local policymakers may not be able to handle without support from higher-level authorities. Third, innovations solve some existing problems but at the same time may create new ones.

Local anti-corruption innovations face both the above problems and difficulties caused by specific local conditions. Thus, exploring the factors that determine why some regions are more likely to take anti-corruption measures than others is interesting. The regional variation of local anti-corruption efforts in China has become a scholarly research focus. Zhu and Zhang (2008) argued that the significant cross-province differences in the corruption cases revealed to the public largely result from the variation in local governments' anti-corruption efforts. They measured local cadres' motivation to fight corruption using two indicators—the number of provincial memberships in the CPC's Central Committee/Politburo and strength of outsider officials (i.e., those appointed by higher levels), and the duration of insider officials (i.e., those promoted from within the province). They concluded that provincially revealed corruption cases positively correlate with the first indicator and negatively with the second (Zhu & Zhang, 2008). Ni and Sun (2015) analyzed anti-corruption data from 21 municipal cities in G Province and confirmed regional disparity in anti-corruption efforts. They found that economic development, decentralization, and the year of the leading municipal cadres' power transition impacted anti-corruption efforts (Ni & Sun, 2015). In general, the extent of economic development positively correlates with local anti-corruption efforts. The greater its decentralization at the municipal level, the less likely a government is to fight corruption. The year of power transition usually sees fewer corruption cases.

2.5 Conclusion

This literature review has focused on China's anti-corruption efforts since the onset of the reform era—including such general questions as the causes and characteristics of corruption, institutional, economic, and organizational approaches to combating corruption, the global trend toward building local integrity systems, and local governments' growing efforts at anti-corruption reform in China—to provide a general picture of China's anti-corruption reform. China is moving away from imposing top-down anti-corruption efforts and towards combining central directives with increased local efforts. Although scholars have had productive discussions on central-level anti-corruption practices, they have not paid sufficient attention to local governments' role in anti-corruption reform. Studies touching upon local reforms mainly discuss local authorities' motivations for conducting anti-corruption innovations; they do not investigate the dilemmas of local innovations. My research focuses on the underlying factors that hold back the sustainability of local innovations and illustrates them through case studies. I also examine the background of local governments' anti-corruption efforts and institutional constraints on China's future efforts to curb corruption.

Notes

1 See Effects Of Corruption On People, Society & Economy, Updated On 13/07/2022 by ranga nr, http://www.mindcontroversy.com/impact-effects-corruption-public-life-india/.
2 United Nations Development Programme (2005): Institutional arrangements to combat corruption, a comparative study, https://www.undp.org/asia-pacific/publications/institutional-arrangements-combat-corruption-comparative-study.

3 Historical Overview

3.1 Revisit Anti-corruption History

Since the founding of the People's Republic of China (PRC) in 1949, the narrative on China's anti-corruption efforts has taken place at a national level and adopted a top-down style, meaning attention has been chiefly paid to China's anti-corruption as a whole, especially anti-corruption moves at the central level (He, 2000; Quade, 2007; Zhu, 2008). Among these narratives, scholars have noticed some paradoxes in China's corruption and social development: rampant corruption has accompanied rapid economic growth since the onset of the reform and opening-up policy in the late 1970s; the government's legitimacy has been undermined by corruption; and how the government used to fight corruption (i.e., campaign-style enforcement) might have actually intensified it (Sun, 2005; Wedeman, 2005). Most studies have emphasized the central government's anti-corruption efforts and impact, while paying inadequate attention to local governments' role (Anechiarico, 2009; Gong, 2014). To better understand local governments' evolving role, we must have background knowledge about China's anti-corruption history. In this chapter, I review China's anti-corruption history since the early 1980s to see if and how a change from top-down to more locally-based efforts has occurred. Recent decades have seen a trend toward local-driven anti-corruption innovation that might breathe fresh air into anti-corruption efforts and differs from past attempts by anti-corruption agencies at all levels in China.

A hot topic in anti-corruption studies is the efficacy of anti-corruption work. Although the Chinese government has engaged in an intense battle against corruption since the beginning of its economic reform in the early 1980s, the effectiveness of its anti-corruption efforts remains questionable. Neither traditional corruption control through *ad hoc* political campaigns, nor organizational purges, nor orthodox moral and political education disseminated through party-state nomenclature have proved effective. Gong & Ren (2013) agreed that anti-corruption efficacy has been far from satisfactory in the past four decades. Though many measures have been taken to combat corruption, corruption remains rampant.

Scholars have offered various explanations for the difficulties China's anti-corruption work has encountered, including a lack of appropriate institutional

DOI: 10.4324/9781003112105-3

designs, rapid economic growth (which provided opportunities for corruption), and the lagging of political reform behind economic reform. Manion (2004) pointed out that without appropriate institutional designs, anti-corruption measures will not stop widespread corruption in China. She mentioned three institutional design features of Hong Kong's anti-corruption efforts from which mainland China could draw lessons: an independent and powerful anti-corruption agency, the social reputation of the anti-corruption agency, and civilizing the masses with the idea of integrity. Wedeman (2005) stated that China has been "trapped in transition," meaning the growing economy has obscured the severity of corruption. He correlated anti-corruption strategies with the stages of China's economic reform, asserting that corruption forms have evolved as the economy has developed. Deng, Zhang, and Leverentz (2010) concluded that without further political reform, corruption is unlikely to be controlled in China. Political reform is a necessary backdrop for more effective anti-corruption agencies.

I intend to illustrate several waves of anti-corruption work and their changing characteristics. Integrity building has undergone several phases, each aimed at different integrity problems that emerged during the corresponding period. A historical review would also help us better understand the current challenges and possible future trends. Looking back on over 60 years of anti-corruption practice in China, we can see the changing foci and features of anti-corruption strategies. To show how the Chinese government has combated corruption in the past four decades, I collected integrity-building rules and regulations from 1979 to now and examined the political and economic background affecting both forms of corruption and corresponding anti-corruption strategies. Attention was given to several key regulations that set detailed standards, pointing to official misbehaviors that occurred frequently and had a significant social impact over a certain period. These rules and regulations illustrate China's changing forms of corruption and evolving anti-corruption strategies and show the differences between anti-corruption stages.

3.2 Trajectory of Anti-corruption Efforts

Scholars agree that China's anti-corruption efforts have evolved through several stages. For example, Gong (2003) divided the process into three phases of anti-corruption policies. The first, involving the founding of the CDIC in 1979 and its provincial branches (1978–1986), focused on Party members; the second phase targeted illegal economic activities, broadening the scope of anti-corruption efforts to include state personnel (1987–1992); the third phase witnessed the intensification of anti-corruption measures targeting more sophisticated forms of corruption (1993–2002). Guo (2008) divided the transitional period into three stages based on the number of corruption cases, the average amount of money involved, and the average latency period of major cases. He found that the average amount of money involved in corruption varied during different periods, rising from 17,000 yuan in the 1978–1990 period, to 2,968,000 from 1991–2000 and 3,208,000 from 2001–2004.[1] Another finding from the collection of cases is that the cumulative number of corruption cases followed an inverted U-shaped trajectory from 1978–2004, rising steadily from under 50 in 1978 to over 250 in 1996 before dropping to under 50 in 2004.[2]

In Guo (2008)'s study, China's economic transition context had different features in each phase. He considered 1978–1990 the first stage because it preceded the strengthening of law enforcement and featured far fewer corruption cases than later phases. The second period was 1991–2000, which featured a sharp increase in major corruption cases following the deepening of reform in 1992. In the third phase (2001–2004) the average latency period of major corruption cases became longer, and the cases themselves became more complex.

I agree that anti-corruption strategies have evolved with changing socio-economic conditions, but take a different analytical angle. I focus more on local efforts' origination and growing engagement and divide the 30-year period into four phases: 1979–1989, 1990–2000, 2001–2010, and 2011–present.

The first phase (1979–1989) was the beginning of China's opening-up and reform period. The 1990–2000 period constituted the second phase, in which China's legal system was restored and began to exercise anti-corruption functions. Deng Xiaoping's 1992 southern speech, in which he emphasized the importance of building a legal system to safeguard economic development, was a milestone in China's reform era, symbolizing a new stage of the reform and opening-up policy and making it clear that economic development and political reform should go hand in hand. The third phase (2001–2010) was distinguished by the 16th National Congress of the CPC, in which a new Party leadership brought significant changes to anti-corruption work, including detailed rules and regulations to control corruption. The fourth phase (2011–present) features enthusiastic local engagement in anti-corruption reform. No longer a top-down process, anti-corruption work features increased local anti-corruption innovations and is heading toward combining top-down and bottom-up anti-corruption efforts.

The following part provides examples and evidence of policy evolution in the four phases. Besides the change of leadership and social conditions mentioned above, the major differences between the phases can be found in the number of regulations and rules enacted, the nature of these regulations, and the extent of decentralization of integrity management power.

Phase I: *Ad hoc* efforts, 1978–1989

The year 1978 has been officially acknowledged as the starting point of China's economic reform. It featured the CPC's Third Plenary Session of the 11th Central Committee, which decided to adopt a national policy of opening China to the outside world and pursuing market-driven economic development. Having gone through the 10-year Cultural Revolution, China was eager to pursue a new political and economic order. At this first stage of reform and opening up, corruption became increasingly prominent, accompanying the country's rapid economic growth. The first decade of marketization witnessed the rise of different forms of corruption China had never experienced before. Various rent-seeking economic crimes appeared, taking advantage of the incomplete market system. Circular No.6 of the CPC's Central Committee for Guiding Party Rectification pointed out two anti-corruption foci: preventing individuals from using their position and power for personal gain, and rectifying irresponsible bureaucratic working styles (Gong, 2003). The 1979 formation of the CDIC may be regarded as a symbolic event indicating the central government's determination to fight corruption.

In the 1980s, a new phenomenon caught the attention of the central government, the proliferation of "administrative enterprises" that engaged in profit-making with direct or indirect government affiliations. A typical case was that of Jin Hui, the deputy director of the general office of the Hubei Party Committee, who took advantage of his official authority to buy state-controlled cars, steel, cement, and other goods and sell them to other enterprises and self-employed entrepreneurs at a profit. At the same time, these enterprises bribed government officials to get privileged access to funding, goods, and operating licenses, bringing them abundant economic benefits. At the end of 1984, official profiteering (*guan dao*) became so rampant that the central government issued the decision to "Prohibit the Party and Government Officials' Engagement in Trade and Business."[3] However, the problem was not resolved. After the "dual-track price system"[4] was introduced in 1985, government officials' engagement in profit-making activities became even more obvious. *Guan dao* became the country's main form of corruption, with the main participants in corruption being "officials who controlled production quotas or import quotas, managers and staff in state-owned companies, and entrepreneurs in non-state enterprises [and colluded] with each other for economic benefits" (Deng et al., 2010: 75).

Accordingly, the CDIC issued some *ad hoc* rules targeting specific corrupt behaviors, including:

1. Duty-related allocation: The CDIC set rules to standardize senior cadres' living conditions to prohibit abuse of duty-related interests and restricted leading cadres' group procurement of living materials.
2. Accepting gifts or other personal benefits: The Central Party Committee forbade government officials from accepting or providing expensive gifts in overseas exchange activities as early as 1980. Central-level government officials and staff were further banned from accepting gifts or other personal benefits in domestic activities in 1988. The CDIC also called for a clean-up of "old-boy" networks (*guan xi hu*).
3. Engaging in for-profit activities and seeking improper interests by abusing one's power: The CDIC and State Council enacted numerous restrictions on government officials' engagement in for-profit activities during the first decade. They mainly aimed at cleaning up government-sponsored

> "private enterprises," prohibiting Party officials' involvement in trading and partnership in running enterprises, and preventing other economic crimes by government officials. The decade witnessed several rectification campaigns, especially from 1982 to 1986, when up to 67,000 people were punished for breaking Party rules.[5]

The main focus of anti-corruption work in this phase was on "*guandao*" and collusion between government officials and businessmen (*guanshang goujie*). Early in 1980, Deng Xiaoping warned that some cadres saw themselves as the public's masters rather than public servants, enjoying privileges that caused strong public dissatisfaction and damaged the Party's image. If the situation could not be changed, China's entire cadre corps would become corrupt.[6] Around the same time, the then General Secretary of the CPC, Hu Yaobang, pointed out that "after coming to power, some of our comrades began to lose their strong revolutionary will and were 'hit by sugar-coated cannonballs,' and got corrupted at the end. This unhealthy tendency would corrupt the body of our Party."[7]

The evolving forms of corruption made it difficult to combat corruption during this period. On the one hand, the incomplete market system continuously gave rise to new forms of corruption. On the other, anti-corruption laws and regulations lagged behind new forms of corruption and were unable to counter them. Before the 1990s, the legal system to support anti-corruption practices barely existed. Deng's 1992 southern speech, which mentioned building a legal system to support economic performance, is evidence of the lack of a legal basis for anti-corruption work before then. Though some general rules existed, they were vague and unspecific and failed to prevent corruption effectively. Ko and Weng (2012) found that neither types of corruption nor punishment levels were specified in the Chinese Criminal Law (hereafter, CCL) issued in 1979, only three types of corrupt behavior: embezzlement, bribery, and neglect of duty (Ko & Weng, 2012). The CDIC enacted some *ad hoc* rules and regulations to solve emerging integrity problems, following the instructions of top leaders.

At this stage, campaign-style anti-corruption efforts were carried out. Wedeman (2005) identified four anti-corruption campaigns (in 1982, 1986, 1989, and 1993, respectively), three of which took place in this period. The campaign-style anti-corruption effort, according to Wedeman (2005: 93), "does not mean equivalent Chinese term '*yundong*'; '*yundong*' has a very particular political meaning—a Maoist-style mass campaign. Contemporary anti-corruption … relies on short bursts of hyper-enforcement by state and Party agencies, wherein the 'masses' are asked to report corrupt cadres but are not allowed to take on an active or leading role, as was the case in a Maoist campaign." Wedeman's evidence was drawn from corruption cases exposed during this period and collectively revealed them to be the intensification of anti-corruption efforts.

Rampant corruption during this stage triggered student demonstrations in June 1989, culminating in the Tiananmen Incident. In a speech soon after the incident, Deng Xiaoping stated that "the third generation of collective leadership should focus on two primary tasks: one is to insist on opening policy, and the second is to punish severe corruption."[8] The Tiananmen Incident was a crisis for the CPC's leadership since it called into question the CPC's legitimacy to rule the country while tolerating severe corruption and not liberalizing China's economy, democracy, and the rule of law. Institution building in anti-corruption work was urgently needed to respond to public demands.

Urgent regulations were enacted to control corruption and change the situation, though still by campaign-style. On August 15, 1989, three major anti-corruption agencies (the Supreme Court, the Supreme Procuratorate, and the National Supervision Ministry) jointly issued an anti-corruption notice[9] requiring all national-level officials who had engaged in bribery, speculation, and other corruption-related crimes to confess to judicial organs within 78 days, during which period propaganda machines were mobilized to urge people to confess (Gong, 2003). It was the first time in the PRC's history that bribe-giving was treated as a crime in the same way as bribe-taking was. The effectiveness of the notice was unprecedented. Party committees, the standing committee of the National People's Congress, and all levels of government offered strong support and did much propaganda work. Reports of corrupt behaviors increased dramatically and a succession of criminal offenders surrendering. Procuratorial and supervisory organs established "report centers" (舉報中心) both at national and local levels. By the end of the 78-day confession period, an estimated 50,000 people had surrendered themselves. The notice represented a peak of anti-corruption in the country. While viewed as successful, the campaign's effectiveness did not last long and corruption continued to rise after it ended.

During the campaign, the procuratorial organs' petition offices received 133,765 reports of embezzlement and bribery, and 25,544 people surrendered money they had received from embezzlement or bribes. Including all categories of economic criminals, 36,171 people confessed and surrendered illegal gains, totaling 209 million yuan. The cadres who surrendered included 742 county-level staff, 40 bureau-level cadres, one deputy provincial-level cadre, and one deputy departmental-level cadre. The marked effects of the notice are more obvious if we compare the figures from before and after its launch. In 1989, the procuratorial organs investigated 58,926 cases of embezzlement and bribery, a 1.8-fold increase from the previous year. Of these, 13,057 were major criminal cases, a 3.4 times increase from 1988, and 875 people were named in key criminal cases, an increase of 3.5 times over the previous year.[10] While the notice was in place, the government also cleaned up many administrative enterprises that had been set up by government institutions. The Xiamen Yuanhua Smuggling Case was the most important case investigated during this period.[11]

From 1989 to 1992, there were 400,000 cases of disciplinary violations, a huge outburst of corruption cases compared to the years before and after. The front-page headline of the July 29, 1989, edition of *People's Daily* listed seven priority anti-corruption measures aimed at stopping abuses of power and prohibiting collusion between government officials and merchants: 1) further rectification of companies; 2) a firm prohibition on cadres' relatives engaging in business deals; 3) cancellation of "special supply" to leading cadres; 4) a strict ban on imported cars for official use; 5) strict prohibitions on accepting gifts; 6) strict controls on cadres going abroad for individual travel with public funds; 7) serious investigations of such crimes as speculation and bribery, and, particularly, recognition of the need to act quickly to investigate major cases. The 1990 creation of the State Council Office for Rectifying (*Guowuyuan jiufeng ban*) further helped the CDIC and State Council focus on severe, long-lasting corruption.

Phase II: Institution building, 1990–2000

Institution building in corruption control is defined as "the proliferation of rules and programs and aims at institutionalising integrity management and promoting government integrity" (Gong, 2011: 672). With this definition, we can better understand the transition from campaign-style anti-corruption enforcement to rule-based integrity building.

Deng Xiaoping's 1992 speech in southern China set the tone for deepening reform and building a corresponding legal system. There appeared to be a near consensus among Chinese leaders that the underlying reason for the ineffectiveness of integrity management was China's lack of institution building. For Deng and other leaders, institution building was meant to carry out anti-corruption reform with the support of laws and regulations. These treatments can be found in the rules mentioned later in this part. Institution building became an important feature of the second phase of the fight against corruption, which separated it from the first phase.

The number of official regulations on integrity management introduced in the 1990s greatly increased compared to the earlier stage (Gong & Ren, 2013). Gong and Ren estimated that 173 regulatory provisions were adopted in the past four decades. They summarized the anti-corruption trend from 1980 to 2009 and found that the number of regulations almost doubled, from 28 in the 1980s to 55 in the 1990s, showing "a clear upward trend, indicating the intensification of integrity management" (Gong & Ren, 2013: 9). At the same time, Chinese society underwent a massive transition, including "decentralization, price reform, greater market penetration, the declining influence of the planned economy, globalization, and privatization of certain state properties" (Deng et al., 2010: 76).

Corruption became increasingly rampant in the context of China's deepening market reform, leading policymakers to emphasize rules and regulations. There were, for example, rules about disciplinary punishment for Party members engaged in economic crimes (1990); the Chinese Communist Party's disciplinary regulations (1997); and the CDIC's regulations punishing those who interfered in the investigation of disciplinary cases (1990). Another important general regulation, Several Integrity Rules for Leading Cadres of the CPC to Follow (*zhongguo gongchandang dangyuan lingdao ganbu lianjie congzheng ruogan zhunze*), which was adopted on a trial basis in 1997 and revised in 2010, specifically prohibited leading cadres from engaging in for-profit activities and using their positions to seek improper interests. Such regulations set new rules for government officials under market economy conditions and held leading cadres to higher standards of ethical behavior.

Phase III: Targeted and specific rules, 2001–2010

The transition from Phase II to Phase III witnessed the further spread of corruption accompanying the deepening of marketization and globalization. Hence, the third stage featured the formulation and implementation of specific rules to fight new corruption.

For several reasons, the 16th National Congress of the CPC in 2002 marked the beginning of the third phase. First, the Party Congress adopted guidelines for anti-corruption work, later referred to as the "16-character guideline" (十六字方針). The guidelines included using both short-term and long-term solutions to deal with corruption (標本兼治), emphasizing punishment and prevention at the same time (懲防並舉), taking comprehensive measures to fight corruption (綜合治理), and focusing on corruption prevention (注重預防). The principle was first proposed by the fourth plenary session of the 16th National Congress to establish and improve the anti-corruption system and make it adaptable to the socialist market economy.

Secondly, the Party Congress emphasized the inner-party inspection system more than ever before, using the phrase "inner-party supervision" for the first time and introducing detailed rules. In 2003, the Central Committee of the CPC issued the Provisional Regulation of Inner-Party Supervision of the CPC, which specified that leading Party cadres at all levels were to be supervised, work in accordance with the Party's rules, abide by the constitution and laws, stick to probity and self-discipline, and contribute to building the Party's integrity. The Party Congress also reformed and improved the Party's discipline inspection system by establishing and enhancing the inspection tour system, and the CDIC and the Central Organization Department (中央組織部) spent five years (2003–2008) setting up a special inspection system. The then Party Secretary, Hu Jintao, reviewed the anti-corruption work in the report of the 17th National Congress and confirmed the achievements of integrity building and clean government.

It was a long way from building these institutional measures to locally-initiated integrity management. The determination of the central government to adopt local innovations led to a tortuous process. The central authorities showed a positive attitude toward local anti-corruption innovations in January 2003. In the third phase, the central leadership focused more on providing detailed instructions to make the rules and regulations practicable. Some of them specified accountability mechanisms and penalties to ensure compliance, which could be seen in the Local DICs' Obligation to Report to the Upper Level about the Integrity Management Situation (enacted in 2003). Some examples include the Provision of Cadres' Self-reporting on Personal Financial Information (2001 and 2010), Regulation of Government Information Disclosure (2008),

Regulation of the Selection and Appointment of Leading Cadres (2002), and Provisional Rules of Cadres' Reporting on Activities (2005). The new decade also emphasized personnel management, state enterprise management, and the construction of a culture of clean government. In 2009, the fourth plenary of the 17th Central Committee passed three new provisions: the implementation of accountability of Party and government leading cadres; the CPC's regulations on the work of inspection tours, and certain rules on the integrity issues of leading cadres of state-owned enterprises.

In the meantime, the development of local innovations became noticeable. Whether local governments should take a more active role in anti-corruption policymaking was a disputed issue in the academic community. Some scholars held that integrity building was a top-down process and controlling corruption should rely on a "top-level design" (頂層設計) (Li, 2013; Ni, 2013; Wang, 2009), meaning central-level policy design was the precondition for effective corruption control. While it is true that the central government is key to establishing a nationwide network of integrity management, there is no denying that local governments' endeavors are strong pillars for more targeted measures and should not be underestimated.

At the CPC's 16th National Congress, the Central Political Bureau proposed that the foci of anti-corruption work would turn to institution building and innovation to prevent and solve the corruption problem from the source.[12] For the first time, the CPC's 16th National Congress proposed to reform the leading system of the Party's discipline inspection department and encouraged the local DICs to explore this reform. One of the most noteworthy articles in the provisional Inner-Party Supervision Regulations of the CPC (中國共產黨黨內監督條例試行) enacted in December 2003 required lower-level DICs to report directly to the upper-level DICs about the significant issues in their regions to avoid the intervention of the Party committee at the same level. This arrangement set up direct reporting channels between the lower- and higher-level DICs and aimed to facilitate efficient information transfer among DICs and to enhance local DICs' authority.

Another development seemed to be a retreat from the 2003 arrangement. The Party Central Committee took back the power to appoint the secretaries of provincial DICs at the CPC's 17th National Congress in 2007. Some provincial-level DIC secretaries were directly appointed by the central level, while others were transferred from other provinces. By retaking the personnel appointment power from provincial DICs, the central government strengthened its top-down cadre management authority.

Phase IV: Local innovations, 2011–present

During this period, a new phenomenon emerged: with the decentralization of integrity management, local governments began to play a more active role in anti-corruption work. They tried out some innovative policies at local levels, though the innovations met different fates due to their various conditions. A transition from top-down anti-corruption practice to a more bottom-up effort was seen. In this paper, the term "bottom-up" is used in the context of the relationship between the central government and local governments.

Local innovations nevertheless progressed in making anti-corruption innovations. Recent years witnessed the initiation and proliferation of local governments' targeted and specific anti-corruption measures. A typical example was the policy (mentioned above) of disclosing personal assets initiated by the Aletai government in Xinjiang in 2009, an idea that had long been discussed among the public before finally being implemented. Following Aletai's step, some Guangdong, Hunan, and Jiangsu local governments took similar measures. Another example was the Integrity Office in Hengqin, Zhuhai, which merged four separate departments (discipline inspection, supervision, procuratorate, and audit) to reset the functions and relationships of government agencies. Many media reports suggested that the practice indicated a higher level of anti-corruption reform, in which local governments played a more active role and enjoyed growing autonomy in taking new measures against corruption.[13]

A subtle change in personnel arrangement also occurred. As local-level anti-corruption reforms grew in importance, the DIC secretary's rank in the Standing Committee of the Party in six provinces (Beijing, Liaoning, Jiangsu, Zhejiang, Hunan, and Guangdong) increased from seventh, eighth, or ninth in importance to fourth, closely following the Secretary and Deputy Secretary of the Provincial Party Committee. This change was broadly reported in the media[14] and implied that the importance of anti-corruption work was growing. More information on recent local-level innovations in integrity management will be discussed in the following part.

Throughout the four phases, the CDIC increased its collaboration with other departments. In the first phase, most rules were formulated by the CDIC and occasionally in conjunction with the State Council. In the second phase, more departments worked with the CDIC, such as the Organization Department of the CPC, the Ministry of Supervision, the Ministry of Finance, the State Economic and Trade Commission, and the Supreme People's Court. Even more departments participated in the rules set in the third stage, including the Ministry of Construction, the Ministry of Land and Resources, the Ministry of Culture, and so on. This trend indicates that the strategies to fight corruption have evolved with the development of corrupt behaviors. Apart from the diversity of anti-corruption methods, it also shows that the CDIC never worked alone and constantly tried to engage more actors in the war against corruption. With the engagement of specialized departments, integrity building became increasingly professionalized. For example, the auditing department conducts professional investigations of the financial operations of governments. This may help promote transparency.

3.3 A Summary of Historical Phases

From the historical review above, we note the impact of the social and economic background on anti-corruption strategies. Marketization was the social background accompanying the history of anti-corruption reform.

The academic community has provided sufficient evidence to show the loopholes in the marketization process gave rise to corruption and brought about different forms of corruption than China had ever experienced before. Hao and Johnston (1995) pointed out the surge of corruption in the early 1990s, while Gong argued that corruption is an unintended and inevitable consequence of China's reform.[15] Guo divided marketization into four stages based on the deepening of marketization (economic liberalization, decentralization, privatization, and globalization) and provided a framework to understand the changing features of corruption (Guo, 2008). In that sense, the anti-corruption history after 1978 could be seen as the fight against the by-product of marketization.

Integrity innovations at local levels work as ways of exploring institution building. These policy innovations require political support from upper-level authorities to be effective and sustainable. Gong summarized the two main reasons why central authorities have encouraged local anti-corruption innovations. First, the central level can neither access all the information that local levels can nor determine whether that information is true or false, making it difficult to get a whole picture of the scope and level of corruption nationwide. Second, local innovations can tailor local policies rather than simply adjust vague national ones (Gong, 2014).

Notes

1 Source: Guo Yong, Corruption in transitional China: an empirical analysis, page 358.
2 Source: Guo Yong, Corruption in transitional China: an empirical analysis, page 357.
3 Why did corruption cases frequently occur in the 1980s? (Shangshiji bashi niandai tanwu fubai weihe jizhong baofa?) June 16, 2011, *People's Daily Online*. http://www.rmlt.com.cn/2011/0622/20638.shtml.
4 The dual-track price system was adopted during the early stage of the transition from the planned economy to a market economy in China (roughly from 1984 to 1989). Production goods had two different prices: a lower price within the planned economy and a higher one in the market economy. This gave rise to the corrupt practice whereby profiteers could get low-priced goods through personal connections in the public sector and sell them on the market for higher prices and private gains. At the time, this kind of behavior was referred to as official speculation ("guandao").
5 The changing anti-corruption mode in the past 60 years (Zhonggong fanfu moshi liushinian bianqian) http://news.qq.com/zt2014/60fanfu/. Accessed in June 2016.
6 Deng's speech on the enlarged meeting of the central political bureau of the CPC, 1980.
7 The national anti-corruption storm in the late 1980s (1980 niandaimo fengbo guohou xianqi quanguoxing lianzheng fengbao). Source: A memory of China in 20th Century, http://www.hybsl.cn/beijingcankao/beijingfenxi/2012-04-20/29451.html Accessed in May 2016.
8 Urgent tasks of China's third generation of collective leadership (June 16, 1989), *Selected Works of Deng Xiaoping*, the third volume, page 313.

9 In accordance with the requirements of the central authority, on August 15, 1989, the Supreme Court, the Supreme Procuratorate, and the National Supervision Ministry jointly held a press conference and issued a notice that national officials who had engaged in bribery, speculation, and other corruption-related crimes must confess to the judicial organs within the following 78 days.

10 See http://www.spp.gov.cn/jcsh/201208/t20120816_5372.shtml. Accessed in June 2015.

11 The Xiamen Yuanhua Smuggling case, may be called "the largest economic case ever in the history of the PRC," attracting wide attention at both home and abroad. The smuggling criminals (represented by Lai Changxing, the head of Yuanhua Group) bribed many government officials, including three provincial and ministerial-level officials and eight departmental-level cadres. According to Xinhua News Agency, the government officials involved in the case were also from the key departments such as the city's Party Committee, municipal government, public security organs, customs, and commercial banks.

12 The innovative development of the CPC's anti-corruption institution building since the 16th National Congress (*Shiliuda yilai zhongguo gongchandang fanfu lianzheng fagui zhidu jianshede chuangxin fazhan*), by Wang Youping http://www.scge.gov.cn/Item/26008.aspx.

13 *Guangzhou Daily* http://fanfu.people.com.cn/n/2012/0910/c64371-18960328.html. Accessed on September 10, 2012; Caixin web http://policy.caixin.com/2012-09-10/100435549.html. Accessed on September 10, 2012; China News Service http://www.jieyue.net/showNews.jsp?classId=UJQP4V8EHQ&newsId=74639 Accessed on September 10, 2012.

14 The secretary of the Discipline Inspection Commission in six provinces ranked fourth and helped deter corruption (*Liu shengfen jiwei shuji paiming lie disi youzhu zhenshe fubai*), *Legal Evening News*, http://news.sohu.com/20140616/n400902996.shtml. Accessed on June 16, 2014.

15 Ting Gong, *The Politics of Corruption in Contemporary China: An Analysis of Policy Outcomes* (Westport, CN: Praeger, 1994).

4 Local Anti-Corruption Innovations

This part will show how the oarsmen, i.e., local governments, play their roles in the anti-corruption battleground, especially in anti-corruption policy innovations. It outlines local governments' efforts in anti-corruption innovations in recent years, revealing they did much innovative work that took rather rich forms. I collected information about 437 local anti-corruption innovations from the official CDIC website.[1] The site is probably the most authoritative website reporting on recent local innovation cases since it reflects the views of the CDIC. These 437 cases were all gathered from the site's "display of local-level anti-corruption innovations (基層風采)" column and cover the period from 2013–2016. The CDIC selected all as good examples of integrity management. Most of these innovations were organized by municipal- or county-level DICs, while a few were by SOEs and provincial DICs. For detailed information on the database, please refer to the appendix. The following part illustrates the geographical distribution, timeline, and features and types of these innovations.

4.1 Local Innovations of this Study

4.1.1 Regional disparity and features

Map 4.1 shows the national geographic coverage of integrity innovations from 2013 to 2016. Of China's 31 mainland provinces (excluding Hong Kong, Macau, and Taiwan), 29 had anti-corruption innovations in recent years, including more developed areas (e.g., the Yangtze River Delta and Pearl River Delta regions) and less-developed areas (e.g., northwestern and southwestern inland areas). The map also illustrates the number of innovations in these provinces, with darker colors indicating more innovations were conducted during 2013–2016.

Based on the above data, the most active innovator provinces were Shandong, Jiangsu, Zhejiang, Jiangxi, Sichuan, and Xinjiang, each with more than 26 major innovation cases during 2013–2016. In contrast, Tibet, Inner Mongolia, Liaoning, and Qinghai each had fewer than four innovations in that period. Most integrity innovations were in east coast areas, while the northeast region was relatively inactive. Xinjiang and Sichuan were the two exceptions in the vast western region. Table 4.1 indicates the specific number of innovations each province conducted during 2013–2016.

DOI: 10.4324/9781003112105-4

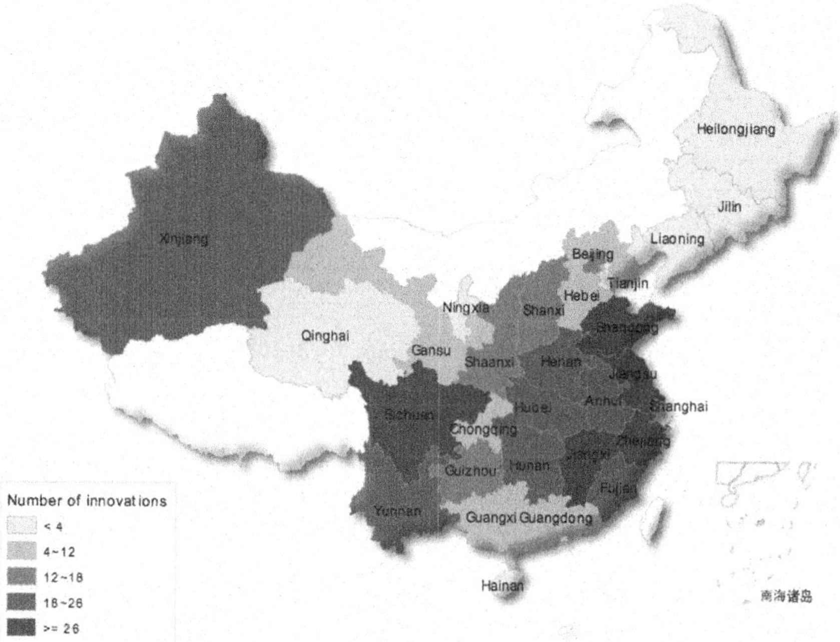

Map 4.1 Number and spread of innovations in provinces

Source: Compiled from the database of local innovations (2013–2016).

Table 4.1 Number of innovations for each province, 2013–2016

Province	*Number of innovations*	*Province*	*Number of innovations*
Jiangsu	43	Guizhou	13
Sichuan	40	Beijing	12
Zhejiang	36	Guangdong	12
Shandong	29	Guangxi	9
Jiangxi	26	Gansu	9
Anhui	22	Hebei	8
Henan	21	Chongqing	6
Fujian	20	Hainan	4
Hunan	20	Jilin	3
Hubei	19	Inner Mongolia	3
Xinjiang	19	Tianjin	2
Yunnan	18	Heilongjiang	1
Shanghai	16	Ningxia	1
Shaanxi	15	Tibet	1
Shanxi	14	Qinghai	0
		Liaoning	0

Source: Compiled by the author from the CDIC dataset, covers 2013–2016.

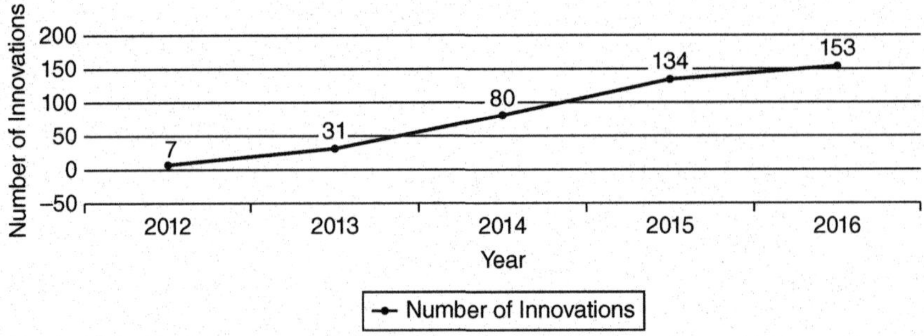

Figure 4.1 A growing trend of local innovations, 2012–2016

Source: Compiled by the author from the dataset from CDIC, 2012–2016.

Another dimension of the dataset is the timing of these innovations. Figure 4.1 shows a growing trend of local innovations in the four years from 2012 to 2016.

As Table 4.2 indicates, the number of innovations has steadily increased each year.

The third analytical dimension is the type of local anti-corruption innovations. By analyzing the innovations' content, we can deduce the local anti-corruption concerns at that time and how local authorities responded to them.

Most observed local-level innovations were related to inner-party supervision. "The Provisional Regulation of Inner-party Supervision of the CPC", issued in 2003, was the first official document concerning the inner-party supervision system in the post-reform period. Subsequently, in October 2016, the CPC's 18th Central Party Committee passed the Regulation of Inner-party Supervision of the CPC.

Table 4.2 Number of innovations each year, 2007–2016

Year	*Number of innovations*
2007	1
2008	1
2009	1
2010	2
2011	2
2012	7
2013	31
2014	80
2015	134
2016	153
From recent years	15

Source: Compiled by the author from the dataset from CDIC, 2007–2016.

Inner-party supervision is defined as the Party's supervision of public employees to keep them from disobeying Party rules and disciplines. Any public employee activities involving public issues fall under inner-party supervision. Inner-party supervision is conducted through a series of actions, such as inspection, evaluation, revealing, and reporting, and includes supervision by Party organizations and mutual supervision among Party members. It also specifies ten measures to strengthen inner-party supervision, which cover collective leadership and division of responsibility, reporting and notification of important conditions, reporting on duties and integrity conditions, democratic life in the Party, handling complaint reporting, making inspection tours, conversation and commandments, supervision by public opinion, answering inquiries from the public, and so on. Innovative anti-corruption policies at the local level are, in most cases, related to inner-party supervision.

Generally, there are two types of anti-corruption innovation: preventing corruption before it happens and controlling it after it occurs. In other words, some innovations are designed to prevent corruption by, for example, reporting potential conflicts of interest, while others are made to warn government officials by educating them about previous corruption cases.

Table 4.3 records a variety of preventive innovation measures. "Pre-corruption innovations" take various forms to prevent corruption from happening. Their topics range from detecting risks of corruption by regularly meeting with cadres on integrity issues, creating various channels to publicize information on integrity, educating cadres about new regulatory redlines for corrupt behaviors, assessing cadres' performance, and holding open dialogues with the public, to conducting disciplinary inspection tours over integrity issues. The table is only a partial list of pre-corruption innovations. The rough number of this type is 205, accounting for nearly half of the innovations studied.

Another group of innovations emphasizes post-corruption measures, including attributing responsibility and holding particular cadres accountable, disclosing corruption cases to increase transparency, and reviewing previous corruption cases to prevent reoccurrence. Post-corruption control measures are far fewer

Table 4.3 Pre-corruption innovations

Topic of innovations	*Number of innovations*
Regularly meeting with cadres on integrity issues	57
Encouraging public reporting on suspected corruption cases	53
Controlling conflicts of interest	41
Assessment of cadres' performance	23
Creating various channels to publicize information on integrity	15
Open dialogue with the public	9
Disciplinary inspection tours (巡察) over integrity issues	7
All	205

Source: Compiled by the author from the database (2013–2016).

Table 4.4 Post-corruption innovations

Topic of innovations	*Number of innovations*
Holding cadres accountable	67
Disclosing corruption cases for more transparency	14
Reviewing previous corruption cases to draw lessons	4
All	85

Source: Compiled by the author from the database (2013–2016).

than pre-corruption innovations, with those listed in Table 4.4 being the most frequently observed. The first type holds cadres accountable by assigning specific responsibilities to particular cadres and monitoring them, mainly targeting corruption cases related to the misuse of poverty alleviation funds, which is frequent at local levels and has a very negative social impact. The second innovation type seeks more transparency by publicizing corruption cases, while the third is educational and involves asking government officials to look at previous cases.

4.1.2 Pattern of innovations

The analysis above indicates various local innovations. The extent to which they are innovative should be further examined. A closer look at the 437 cases in my database reveals three kinds of initiatives: those aiming to make central policies more specific and more suitable for local conditions, those adopting updated technologies or instruments to implement central policies or regulations, and those developing new ideas and methods to control and prevent corruption. Table 4.5 provides a detailed summary.

Table 4.5 Three types of innovations

Types of activity	*Characteristics*	*Examples*
Implementation of the central policies	Make specific rules under the general policies of the central government.	Design detailed rules for disciplinary inspections of the local DICs, which are a localized version of the central rules set in 2004.
Application of new technologies	Update policy instruments without institutional change.	Using special media such as *wechat*, *sina weibo* to connect with the public, creating indicator systems to evaluate cadre performance, and establishing databases to monitor corruption cases.
Innovative experiments	New anti-corruption methods without central instruction or sample practice offered by others.	Reconstructing anti-corruption agencies for more autonomy, setting up integrity account for cadres to hand in grey money, joint anti-corruption activities between local governments.

Source: Compiled by the author from the database (2013–2016).

The first type extends central policy to the local level and is treated as a type of local innovation, because local governments must adapt central policies to local conditions. A common way is to make more detailed rules under the general rule published by the central government. For example, detailed rules for inspections of local DICs are a localized version of the central rules set in 2004. The DIC of Yili prefecture of Xinjiang launched its first round of inspection tours in March 2016, targeting the Commercial Office of Yili and the Management Center of the Housing Pension Fund of Yili, respectively. The inspector group announced a hotline telephone number for informants to report malfeasance and provide relevant clues. All these efforts were under the framework of the 2004 national rule.

In Nanjing, another attempt to put central rules into local practice was made in November 2015. The Jiangning district government of Nanjing organized an annual review of local cadres' integrity performance, subject to the Rule of Honesty and Self-discipline of the Party Members (中國共產黨廉潔自律準則) and the Disciplinary Regulations of the CPC (中國共產黨紀律處分條例) issued by the Central Party Committee. These innovations ran no risks but followed what the central government requested.

The second type is innovative in that they adopt new technologies to enhance anti-corruption effectiveness. The innovations of this type are analogous to putting old wine in new bottles, i.e., taking on new forms to encourage people's reporting of corruption cases and conduct integrity education for both officials and the public. However, the innovation does not include institutional reform. Typical forms of this type use technical improvements in anti-corruption work, including setting up indicator systems to evaluate cadre performance, establishing databases to monitor corruption, and making responsibility lists for cadres to follow. Other means include releasing information online and getting public feedback, building integrity education centers/museums, opening official WeChat/Weibo accounts, and encouraging the public to report corruption cases.

For example, the DIC of Suzhou registered its official *weibo* account (Lianshi Voice/廉石聲音) on *Sina* in February 2013 and now has over 140,000 online followers, half of whom are active users. The *Weibo* account serves as a communication channel between the DIC and people concerned about integrity management in Suzhou. A second example of this type of innovation happened in Zhuhai in March 2016, when the municipal government established an online system for real-time supervision of officials by digital means. New digital technology helps clarify officials' responsibilities, traces the working process with real-time monitoring, and warns about behaviors that carry corruption risks as early as possible. The system also facilitates collecting and analyzing data and getting first-hand information on local officials' activities.

The third type involves local experiments with innovative elements that are new even to the central government. The innovators in these cases did not borrow recipes from other localities and usually got no central government input until the innovation showed signs of success and attracted the attention of higher authorities. For example, some local governments aimed at reorganizing government institutions to enhance local anti-corruption watchdogs' role in corruption prevention and integrity management. Another example is anti-corruption collaboration among local governments, such as the North Bay Forum on Clean Government, where border cities in three provinces (Guangdong, Guangxi, and Hainan) collaboratively promote cross-regional cooperation and supervision to prevent corruption (Gong, 2014).

From the above discussion, it is clear that although local governments have made numerous innovations in integrity management in recent years, they have mostly remained at a nascent stage. While the central government makes general policies and regulations for the whole country, their local implementation can be difficult as they must be adjusted to be feasible at grassroots levels. In essence, the central government draws rough outlines to be followed and local governments create detailed versions thereof. One common feature of innovation cases is that they closely follow inspiration from the central government. Specifically, local DICs most frequently observed topics are highly congruent with central government intentions: the Eight-Point Regulations (八項規定) against the abuse of public expenditures, clarifying the main responsibilities of Party committees (主體責任), controlling four kinds of corrupt behaviors (反四風), etc. As stated above, the second type did not go far enough toward institutional change. My study focuses on the third type only, because it is meaningful for future research and practically significant for China's local integrity building. However, this does not imply that the other two types are insignificant.

4.2 Four Cases: An Overview

Case I: Innovation without social support

The first case is the Integrity Pension Fund in Jiangmen (*lianzheng gongjijin*), from 2010. The policymakers' original intention was to enhance civil servants' integrity through economic incentives. The Integrity Pension Fund was an economic tool encouraging civil servants to keep corruption away. Civil servants who volunteered to join the fund would deposit part of their monthly salaries into their pension accounts and have it matched by public expenditure. The civil servant could receive 70% of the fund every five years if their activities followed Party regulations and disciplines and the remainder if they abided by the integrity rules until retirement; otherwise, the fund would revert to the state treasury. However, after the policy was implemented in 2010, it received harsh public and mass media criticism, leading the provincial DIC to abolish the Jiangmen Pension Fund only three months after it was enacted. This case shows how a lack of social support may lead to an absence of political support.

Case II: Innovation without organizational support

The second case concerned the integrated Office of Integrity (*lianzheng bangongshi*) in Zhuhai Hengqin founded in September 2011 as China's first multi-function integrity office. The Hengqin case attempted to bring four branches—the discipline inspection committee, supervision department, procuratorate, and audit agencies—into one body. Suspicions about the effectiveness of China's current anti-corruption agencies, particularly their insufficient independence, informed the logic underlying the integrated integrity office. As the main player among integrated anti-corruption agencies, the discipline inspection committee works jointly with other agencies, such as the supervision, procuratorate, and audit departments. The Integrated Office of Integrity was expected to function as an independent ACA, as the ICAC in Hong Kong is supported by the Guangdong DIC. However, this effort has met strong objections, with critics claiming that putting the procuratorial department under the DIC management may be unconstitutional.

> *Due to the weakness of the legal system (the lack of appropriate contract and company laws, the unfamiliarity with such laws and the apprehension that these laws may be subject to changes or to re-interpretations), the legal enforcement of contracts is unreliable.*
>
> (Schmieding, 1991)

Underlying this criticism is the conflict of institutional interests among different departments. Breaking inherent institutional arrangements and merging them into one office is challenging and requires organizational support to achieve coherent collaboration from all departments involved. Currently, the Integrity Office is still making efforts and attempts to survive the various challenges, but its future remains uncertain.

I conclude from the case of the Integrated Office of Integrity in Zhuhai, Hengqin, that an anti-corruption innovation would never succeed absent sufficient organizational support. In the Hengqin case, the Chinese Constitution does not permit integrating the local DIC and procuratorate. While this institutional void hinders the Hengqin government's efforts to establish an effective Office of Integrity, it is not the fatal factor in deciding the fortune of the innovation. The Hengqin Integrated Office of Integrity will manage to survive as long as sufficient political support remains.

Case III & Case VI: Innovation with sufficient institutional support

The third case is the Qianhai Anti-corruption Bureau (QAB), which resembles the Hengqin Integrity Office in its efforts to establish a relatively independent local anti-corruption agency. It has largely functioned well and shows signs of continuity. The Qianhai Case proves that the nature of anti-corruption innovations matters less than their level of institutional support.

Similar to Hengqin, the QAB attempted to merge the DIC, auditing, supervision, public security, and procuratorate bodies into three departments: investigation, corruption prevention, and community work. Though having almost the same reform contents as the Hengqin Case, it has functioned more smoothly, mainly due to its overall institutional support, especially from other concerned organizations. The QAB personnel were under the direct management of the Shenzhen Municipal government, allowing it to avoid departmental conflicts from the beginning; in the case of the QAB, the IMO was challenged by the procuratorate department until they ended with separation.

The fourth case is the reform of government vehicle management (*gongche gaige* 公車改革) in Shenzhen. Government vehicles are a chief component of three public expenditures (*sangong xiaofei* 三公消費) that have become increasingly extravagant and drawn broad public criticism. Shenzhen was one of the first cities to introduce reforms aimed at reducing the abuse of government vehicles and saving public expenditures.[2] More specifically, the vehicle management reform in Shenzhen set a clear goal of 10% savings in public expenditure by cutting down on the number of vehicles owned by government units. Government officials are encouraged to use public transportation and receive financial subsidies for doing so. The policy has affected most officials, and while some are unhappy about losing the power to use government vehicles as they like, the innovation has been successful. It has been carried out under a valid legal framework, has obtained higher authorities' support, and has become widely accepted by the public.

In sum, these four cases have their own characteristics, target various policy areas, and have very different fates. The first focuses on the independence of an anti-corruption agency, the second on building integrity incentives, and the third and fourth on effective integrity management. Among the four, one has failed, a second is being carried under great difficulty, and the last two has been relatively successful. These cases show the complexity and difficulty of policy innovation, even with relatively high local autonomy.

4.3 Institutional Void as an Analytical Framework

4.3.1 The concept of "institutional void"

The term "institutional void" originated from marketing research and has been applied to other research areas. Hajer coined its most widely recognized definition in 2003, saying an "institutional void" means having no accepted rules and norms based on which politics can be conducted and policy measures agreed upon (Hajer, 2003: 175). "Institutional voids," the phrase used by Khanna in his book "Winning in Emerging Markets," refers to the absence of intermediaries such as market research firms and credit card systems to efficiently connect buyers and sellers (Khanna, 2013: 15). For Khanna, understanding these voids—and learning how to work with them in specific markets—is the key to success.

An institutional void can then be understood as "the absence of strong market and legal institutions" (Luo & Chung, 2012), an "unstable institutional setting" (Yep, 2015), or "the complete absence [and] inadequacies of existing institutional set-ups" (Ngo, 2015). In a more detailed way, it is taken as the absence of any of the following: 1) the role of government, more particularly the fight against corruption, illiteracy, and poverty; 2) the rule of law, including issues of accountability, transparency, and citizen rights; and 3) regulation of processes of accountability and oversight for public-private partnerships and citizen involvement (Michels & Montfort, 2013: 1). Generally speaking, "[a] void exists when the predominant institutional infrastructure cannot provide sufficient regulatory or coordinating functions essential to social interactions" (Ngo, 2015: 102).

Scholars on this subject believe that an institutional void usually exists in underdeveloped political or economic institutional settings, and their main focus is finding out how to fill it. An institutional void, by their definition, leaves room for social and state negotiation and reaching a certain consensus. Sometimes, voids may bring about opportunities that could be preconditions for new policies and institutions.

4.3.2 Institutional void in public administration research

The institutional void has been gradually adopted in public administration and political science research after extensive application in marketing research. Scholars have applied the theory of institutional void to all kinds of topics in public administration, including but not limited to the study of developing countries (Ngo, 2009), social movements (Ngo, 2015), local management (Yep, 2015), and democratic transitions (Bedock, 2013). These studies all focus on societies undergoing transitional economic or political reforms, where corruption and increasing social and economic inequalities caused by institutional voids could be destabilizing factors and undermine the collective interests of and sustainable and productive partnerships between the state, the market, and civil society (Michels & Montfort, 2013: 19). Institutional voids need to be filled with social transformation because newly emerging practices require rules and standards to. For example, Ngo et al. (2011) discussed institutional voids in East Asian developing countries because "it is an established wisdom that institutions matter in development, most developing economies are characterized by the absence of much-needed institutional arrangements to regulate market exchange, mobilize economic resources, and coordinate social activities," and pointed out the importance of filling institutional voids. Institutional voids can be filled by unconventional actors/organizations by negotiating rules, resources, and discourses with formal and informal circuits of power; consequently, alternative forms of governance may emerge.[3] The reliability and credibility of new institutions played a significant role in the post-Soviet social transformation, though the government did not know from the outset whether the new institutions were best suited to the intended policies (Schmieding, 1991). Yep indicated the possibility of spontaneous grassroots-level institutional change to fill an institutional void by presenting a case in which society-state interactions led to a compromise in a dispute over rural land use in China. Given the ever-changing nature of land institutions at the top, there is always space to renegotiate the institutional parameters created by the central decisionmakers (Yep, 2015).

The studies mentioned above view institutional void as providing opportunities for new institutions. A lack of an institution creates a window of opportunity for compensatory innovations. Scholars studying policymaking in an institutional void setting have found double dynamics between filling institutional voids and newly emerging institutions: "actors not only deliberate to get to favorable solutions for particular problems but while deliberating they also negotiate new institutional rules, develop new norms of appropriate behavior and devise new conceptions of legitimate political intervention" (Hajer, 2003: 176). Ferraro et al. (2012) conceptualized institutional voids as opportunities for entrepreneurial actors who are motivated to address them. They summarized creating new institutions as "institutional fabric inchoate" (Ferraro et al., 2012: 1). For example, new policies have come from an absence of good governance, leading to public-private coproduction, social enterprises, and so forth. Institutional void thus allows new forms of social service provision to appear as remedies for the state's absence in the area. Stephan, Uhlaner, and Stride (2015) agreed that "[s]ocial enterprises frequently appear where governments fail to provide for social needs such as adequate health care, children's social services, or environmental protection."

Among the scholars who have studied institutional voids, "[a]lmost all have devoted considerable research effort to discussing the limitations of their present institutional arrangements and how they might be changed" (Bedock, 2013: 36). However, scholars have failed to agree on what is meant by "institutional void," a widely-used term whose interpretation depends on scholars' particular concerns and contexts. It remains unclear what exactly voids are, how they have been created, and what causes them. If these questions remain unanswered, it will be difficult to overcome institutional voids.

4.4 The Analytical Framework

In essence, institutional voids occur whenever "supporting institutions" do not exist and policy efforts, consequently, meet challenges.[3] "Institutional void" in this research refers to the lack of political, organizational, and social foundations for a new policy initiative. Institutional support is the key to the success of innovations. Although innovations may occur, get prorated, or even diffused, they would not last long without the support of strong institutional foundations. As pointed out by Van de Ven, the process of innovation is the development and implementation of new ideas by people who, over time, engage in transactions with others within an institutional context. To understand the innovation process is to understand the ideas, people, transactions, and context of the innovation (Van de Ven, 1986: 591). It could be applied to administrative kinds of innovations in this research. Now I will comb the literature on the relationship between innovation and three types of support to further demonstrate the analytical framework.

4.4.1 Innovation and political support

The first is political support for innovation, referring to legal and political support from upper-level authorities, i.e., whether the innovation is within the framework of the legal system and permitted by higher authorities. As has been pointed out by the scholars mentioned above, the legal void is part of the institutional void, referring to "the absence of strong legal institutions" (Luo & Chung, 2012), or "the inadequacy of the rule of law" (Michels & Montfort, 2013: 1). Legal support is essential to innovations, as policy attempts will suffer or fail if they do not fit existing legal parameters. Innovation may emerge in a bottom-up fashion; however, it is difficult for policy innovations to survive or be sustained without superior top-down support. This is particularly true in China's context, where the blessing or endorsement of central upper-level authorities is key to local innovations' success. There is also a wide consensus that a supportive, collaborative, and participative leadership style (transformational) is more likely to encourage innovation within an organization than transactional leadership styles (Kanter, 1983).

Political support could even be regarded as the chief foundation of administrative innovations in China. One myth in innovation studies concerns how political support originated in innovations. Conventional wisdom holds that not enough top-down motivation exists to support innovation in the public sector, according to public choice theory, for the following reasons: first, the public sector is usually a monopoly, with no competitive pressure to innovate; second, the public sector has stable and consistent tasks and resists change or disruption of these tasks. However, recently the situation has been changing because the public sector is facing challenges and opportunities (Borins, 2002: 467).

I agree with this burden-reaction approach to explaining political support for innovations in China. If we look into the Award of Local Innovations, one common feature of the rewarded innovations is that they were created to solve emergent conflicts at the grassroots level. For example, Wu et al. (2013) concluded that most innovations that win the Award aim to improve government management and public service provision and, thereby, solve social problems and settle social disputes. This finding further confirms the "burden-reaction" approach to explaining the motivations behind local innovations. Wu et al. (2013) pointed out that there have been more innovations at the municipal and county levels than at the provincial level, affirming the conventional wisdom that innovations usually take place at lower levels to settle grassroots-level problems. Thus, burden-reaction is local leaders' main motivation for supporting such innovations.

4.4.2 Innovation and organizational support

The second is organizational support, which is measured by the cohesiveness of a given organization. Organizational support means that the organization works as a team to conduct an innovation. Unlike political and social support, organizational support is an internal factor for innovation. In return, innovations also have something to do with the power of bureaucracy and, broadly speaking, a loyal and professional bureaucratic system.

Baldridge and Burnham (1975) made a relatively early attempt at discovering the relationship between organizational characteristics and the likelihood of innovation. They held that structural characteristics of the organization, such as size and complexity, strongly affect its innovative behavior. In most situations, increased size and complexity are expected to lead to increased innovation.

Montes et al. confirmed the hypothesis that organizational cohesion is positively associated with innovation performance (Montes, Moreno, & Morales, 2005). Eisenberger et al. (2001: 42) provided further evidence for this view from a psychological approach that holds that perceived organizational support (POS) impacts employees' organizational commitment and job performance. They found that POS is positively related to employees' perceived obligation to care about the organization's welfare and help it reach its objectives; the employees' perceived obligation mediates the associations of POS with affective commitment, organizational spontaneity, and in-role performance.

4.4.3 Innovation and social support

Social support is the third condition. Innovation with social support is socially constructed and culturally embedded (Raffaelli & Glynn, 2015). The idea of innovation may come out of a few policy entrepreneurs, but innovations must be socially understood and endorsed. In other words, how they can benefit society at large should be made clear to the general public. A social innovation without a social foundation is doomed to fail.

First, local innovations have to be socially constructed. "They are shrouded in legitimated meanings, socially constructed from the values they embody or the cultural configurations that they appropriate or that embed them" (Raffaelli & Glynn, 2015: 21). Second, local innovations must absorb relevant cultural resources from broader contexts that enable interpretation and implementation (Raffaelli & Glynn, 2015: 16). Local innovations vary with locations and must adapt to different cultures rooted in those places.

What follows is how to foster innovation with sufficient social support. The innovators should better absorb the symbols, discourse, and customs from social and cultural environments and foster tailor-made innovations. They are also urged to make public voices heard in policymaking.

4.4.4 Institutional constraints for local innovations

In this study, I select four innovative cases to demonstrate how institutional voids hold back local-level innovations or, more specifically, how the lack of political, structural, and social support impedes local innovations. The cases include the formulation of an integrated Office of Integrity in Zhuhai Hengqin, the establishment of Qianhai Anti-corruption Bureau (QAB), the experiment of the Integrity Pension Fund in Jiangmen, and the reform of government vehicle management in Shenzhen. These four cases were chosen for comparison to help illustrate the impact of institutional voids on the ultimate destiny of different innovations.

Innovations are made by local governments, which receive both top-down instruction and bottom-up supervision, as they have to find solutions for social problems that would satisfy the higher authorities and the public. Local governments try to strike a balance between the intentions of higher authorities and the needs of the public, which may sometimes conflict, as will be shown in my case studies. The first step in understanding how local governments design and implement innovative policies in such a dilemma is to find the institutional obstacles that turn local governments away from successful innovations. However, as I mentioned in the review of the literature on factors that lead to successful innovations, I will not stop at looking for institutional voids for innovations, but will further identify the conditions under which local governments react to the voids. Some local innovations cannot survive the challenge caused by institutional voids; others are struggling with voids; still others have overcome them.

4.5 Conclusion

The review in this chapter suggests that local innovations are necessary and the localization of anti-corruption methods and solutions is beneficial. China is a giant country with substantial local differences. There is a joke about policymaking and implementation in China that "the central command cannot go farther than Zhongnanhai" (政令不出中南海). This may be somewhat true because central command cannot work well at local levels without adaptations to local situations. Local governments should make innovative policies that fit local realities because no one owns better local knowledge than they do, making local innovations worth encouraging and studying. However, the third type of innovation—local experiments with innovative ideas—is rare at the current stage. Many current innovations are of the first two types as they run much less risk, and following the central level's instructions or intentions may lead to their being rewarded by higher authorities.

The context of this research is that whereas almost everyone wants to be an innovator, no model exists for them to follow. Innovators are making attempts and running risks at the same time. Innovation usually means adding more burdens to existing administrative matters, potentially bringing about public misunderstandings and challenges and touching the bottom line of laws and regulations. This research realizes the necessity of local anti-corruption innovations and aims to answer the most puzzling questions that local governments face in making innovations. The significance of this study is to determine the most efficient way to achieve a successful innovation or at least describe under what institutional conditions an innovation has the greatest chance to advance and achieve the innovators' original goals.

Notes

1 http://www.ccdi.gov.cn/gzdt/jcfc/index.html.
2 The reform policy of government vehicle management has been making pilots all over the country lately. There existed three modes: the first approach is to pay back a subsidy; the second one is to redistribute the government vehicles and take back the extra ones; and the third approach is the combination of the above modes. The current central policy adopts the third one, to cancel the general public transport and provide a certain subsidy to civil servants according to administrative levels. The local governments are now introducing local policies that fit the actual situation.
3 See Symposium "Institutional Voids and the Governance of Developing Economies", 16 May 2011, https://www.iias.asia/event/institutional-voids-and-governance-developing-economies.

5 The Jiangmen Case

5.1 Integrity Pension Fund

The first case is the Integrity Pension Fund in Jiangmen. The Integrity Pension Fund is similar to the current housing fund implemented in China, which is familiar to Chinese people. "Housing fund" refers to a long-term fund accumulated by employees in SOEs (State-Owned Enterprises 國有企業), government organs, private enterprises, and NGOs (Non-Government Organizations 非政府組織) for purchasing a house. It comprises two parts, one charged to the working unit the employee belongs to, the other to the employee. Unlike the housing fund, the Integrity Pension Fund only applies to government officials. One thing common to both is that the composition of the fund comes from individuals and organizations: the housing fund pool from certain individuals and enterprises, and the Integrity Pension Fund from the government official and some public expenditure. Those not found to have broken any regulation or law can withdraw a certain proportion of the fund regularly after retirement. Those disobeying the rules must return a portion of the fund to the State treasury.

The Integrity Pension Fund is a financial tool encouraging civil servants to eschew corruption. A great challenge for policymakers is to make this innovative policy feasible by detailing which proportion of the fund is awarded or used as punishment and the conditions for canceling or receiving the fund. A clear design is essential to ensure a policy works well. Only through well-functioning innovation can the scheme achieve the policymakers' original intention, i.e., to motivate government officials to remain honest.

The policymakers were motivated to achieve this innovation in mainland China by learning how Hong Kong enhanced its civil servants' integrity through economic incentives. Hong Kong is known worldwide for its excellent performance in integrity management, steadily ranking around 15 in the Corruption Perception Index in recent years.[1] As one of the least corrupt regions in the world, Hong Kong has a series of institutions and policies to encourage its civil servants to remain honest, including but not limited to high salaries, regular wage increases, and good welfare treatment. Based on Bureau of Civil Service data, civil servants' salaries and related expenses were 89.4 billion yuan in 2013–14, accounting for 26.48% of government expenditure, a relatively high proportion

DOI: 10.4324/9781003112105-5

in global terms.[2] Furthermore, civil servants in Hong Kong enjoy competitive welfare treatment, as stated on the official website of the Hong Kong Bureau of Civil Service, including free medical care at public hospitals (including family members), reasonable vocational policy, and monthly housing benefits (e.g., receiving a housing allowance equal to one-third of one's monthly salary when purchasing a private house, or getting preferential access to public housing).[3]

The Integrity Pension Fund of Hong Kong, which has been in effect since 2003, informed the Jiangmen Case. The scheme includes mandatory and voluntary contributions from civil servants and the government of Hong Kong. Civil servants must contribute 5% of their salary to the fund but may voluntarily contribute more. The government's contribution, calculated based on the civil servant's uninterrupted service years, ranges from 5% to 25% of the servant's salary, see Table 5.1 below.

Civil servants may take money from the Integrity Pension Fund when they leave their public positions. However, the fund has clear punishment policies allowing the government to take back or deduct its contributions if civil servants violate integrity rules or regulations or suspend fund payments when investigating someone's behavior. The 2010 revision of the Civil Servants' Management Command (公務人員管理命令) lists three levels of punishment and penalty, ranging from heavy to light. In Level 1, if one is removed from office, all government contributions to the fund are taken back; at Level 2, if one is forced to retire, a maximum of 25% of government contributions can be deducted; and at Level 3, if one is forced to retire, there will be no deduction of government contribution.[5]

In 2003, Liuyang City of Hunan Province made the first attempt to adopt the Integrity Pension Fund policy in mainland China. Two years later, in January 2005, Xiacheng District of Hangzhou City and Cixi City experimented with this policy, but both received harsh public criticism. Thus, the original plan to further implement the Integrity Fund was delayed. In Guangdong Province, Shenzhen City tried to set up an Integrity Pension Fund in 2003 but terminated it in 2004 due to wide condemnation.[6]

Table 5.1 Hong Kong government's rate of contribution into the fund

Years of employment	*Rate of Hong Kong government's contribution into the fund*
Below three years	5%
3–15 years	15%
15–20 years	17%
20–25 years	20%
25–30 years	22%
Over 30 years	25%

Source: Bureau of Civil Service, Hong Kong.[4]

The Liuyang Integrity Pension Fund has followed a zigzag course, with the most recent public information about it being contained in a 2013 media report. Eleven years after its implementation, the number of government officials covered by the fund was 1,600, most of whom were at or above the sector level. Cumulatively, 57 civil servants had violated laws or regulations, resulting in 164,300 yuan being reclaimed from the fund.[7] For Hangzhou and Cixi, no follow-up information could be found online since the policy was implemented.

The Jiangmen case was chosen for a case study for several reasons. First, Jiangmen was one of the earliest cities to make this innovation, though it was not the only locality to attempt to implement an integrity pension fund policy.[8] Though it turned out to be a failure, the Jiangmen Case provides lessons for policymakers to apply in other cases. Second, the Jiangmen case received the most attention on social media and had a great social impact. Among the relevant cases, the Jiangmen case is the most widely reported by mainstream media and raised both heated social discussion and political attention from upper-level DICs. Third, the case followed a dramatic course. It began smoothly, enjoying the support of the provincial DIC, but ended embarrassingly, with the Guangdong DIC ordering its termination. Hence, the following section will illustrate different stages of the case, determine how the actors interacted, and identify why it finally became a policy failure.

5.2 An Introduction to the Jiangmen Case

Jiangmen, a prefecture-level city on the western Pearl River Delta in Guangdong Province of southern China, had a population of about 4.48 million in 2015. In Chinese, Jiangmen means the gate of a river. The city got this name because it looks like a gate with two giant mountains facing each other and a giant river (the Pearl River 珠江) flowing between them. Jiangmen's economic performance is above average; in 2015, it ranked ninth among Guangdong's 21 cities, with a total GDP of 231.1 billion and a GDP growth rate was 8.3%.[9]

The Scheme of Integrity Pension Fund in Jiangmen was activated in 2010. Learning from the Integrity Pension Fund in Hong Kong, the civil servants who volunteered to join the fund paid a part of their monthly salaries into the fund that was matched by public expenditures. Pension members could receive 70% of the fund every five years if none of their activities broke laws or disciplines and all accumulated funds if they did not break integrity rules until retirement. Otherwise, the fund would be donated to the state treasury.

However, simply copying Hong Kong's Integrity Pension Fund Scheme did not fit the mainland context. The first barrier was the different salary management systems between Hong Kong and mainland China. Unlike the relatively high pay system in Hong Kong, mainland China's civil servant pay system has been stalled, with civil servants complaining for years about low salary increases. Also, the public could by no means accept a dramatic increase in civil servants' pay.[10] Thus, we may find that the risk to this innovation was rooted in the pay system for civil servants in mainland China. While the policymakers' intention may have been good, it was hard for the public to understand, especially when it was undertaken in a relatively developed area, Jiangmen of Guangdong Province.

5.2.1 Timeline of the innovation

In 2010, the money going into the Integrity Pension Fund pool came equally from government officials (personal-level) and municipal-level (organizational-level) fiscal expenditures from Jiangmen City's annual budget. At that time, there were 4,600 municipal-level government officials, and the estimated fiscal expenditure for this scheme was 20 million yuan for the first five-year period. No funds were allowed to be withdrawn for personal use during these five years, and government officials could only withdraw their full funds after retirement.[11]

The Integrity Pension Fund was voluntary for the more than 4,600 civil servants working in municipal government offices. Those facing economic difficulty or who viewed it as unnecessary were not compelled to participate. However, participation was compulsory for those above the level of Deputy Section Chief.[12]

The scheme also clarified that government officials could get all their integrity funds back when they retired. After retirement, if any misconduct had been detected during their working years, their retirement salary would be reduced by the regulated proportion.

Interviews revealed that the policymakers made sufficient preparations for this scheme, spending over two years preparing for the policy innovation. In June 2008, the Municipal Party Committee and the municipal government of Jiangmen sent a joint research group to Liuyang City in Hunan Province to gather information and learn from them. After the fieldwork trip, the policymakers held a frank discussion with municipal Party committee members. Chen Jixing, then the Party Secretary of Jiangmen, affirmed this scheme as a policy innovation that could be pioneered in Guangdong Province.[13]

The introduction of the Integrity Pension Fund can be divided into three stages: preparing for the policy; making specific rules for the Integrity Pension Fund; and improving relevant measures. Eventually, the fund received harsh public criticism and was terminated shortly after its implementation. Table 5.2 shows some of the main events of the Jiangmen case.

Table 5.2 Timeline of the Jiangmen case

Time	*Issue*
May 2008	The scheme of Integrity Pension Fund was proposed.
June 2008	Investigation group was sent from Jiangmen to Liuyang.
April 2009	The public expenditure established for the Integrity Pension Fund was listed on the financial budget of 2010.
January 2010	The Fund was written into the annual report of Jiangmen by the Municipal Party Secretary.
July 2010	Implementation of Integrity Pension Fund.
October 2010	Termination of Integrity Pension Fund by the provincial DIC.

Source: compiled by the author from interviews and media reports.

The start of the Integrity Pension Fund in Jiangmen can be traced back to May 2008. Based on an interview of the innovation's policymakers, the Integrity Pension Fund scheme was the most innovative of 19 Jiangmen municipal Party committee research topics and was expected to go further in political reform. It ran a correspondingly higher risk but had sufficient initial political support. Government officials in Jiangmen DIC learned about the scheme from home and abroad and took advice from the People's Congress, the Chinese People's Political Consultative Conference (CPPCC), civil servant representatives, and public representatives, most of whom agreed to the scheme. The Jiangmen DIC government officials went to Jiangsu (Nanjing), Zhejiang, and Hunan to conduct fieldwork and reported their idea and work plan to the provincial leadership. After that, in April 2009, the Fund was discussed repeatedly, first in the enlarged meeting (擴大會議) of Jiangmen's standing committee and then at the municipal government's executive meeting. The public expenditure established for the Integrity Pension Fund was listed in the financial budget of 2010.

Jiangmen City organized all related departments to ensure the policy's smooth implementation. The key was a special management organization supervised by the DIC of Jiangmen. Jiangmen City also reached an agreement with the agency bank to deal with the bank accounts. Other backup departments, such as the auditing department and the financial bureau, were in charge of routine auditing and managing the funding, respectively. The policy designers established regulations stating the scheme was voluntary and requiring participants to sign their names to show their willingness. In principle, those above the Deputy Section Level (副科級) were expected to participate as pioneers; however, as the policy was not mature, the regulation's wording was changed from "should" to "might as well." In reality, it was a political task to be achieved by those above the level.

In January 2010, the then Mayor of Jiangmen, Wang Nanjian, mentioned integrity building in his annual working report. He emphasized that "institutions to prevent and combat corruption should be set up. To go one step further from combating corruption toward keeping government officials away from the root of corruption." Specifically, the institution aimed to strictly control government vehicle expenditures, meetings, official receptions, official business trips abroad, and other regular office expenses. Besides proposed integrity schemes, such as a mechanism for disclosing integrity information in rural areas, he also stressed the Integrity Pension Fund as worth exploring to demonstrate a lack of tolerance toward corruption.

Table 5.3 shows the nine levels for government officials' deposits into the fund, based on their positions.

Based on the "CPC Disciplinary Regulations" (*Zhongguo gong chan dang jilu chufen tiaoli*/中國共產黨紀律處分條例), those who broke the rules would be punished by losing part or all of their funds. As seen in Table 5.4, Jiangmen made a more detailed punishment policy referring to the Hong Kong Integrity Pension Scheme.

Table 5.3 Standard of pay put into the fund, based on administrative levels

Position	*Personal contribution/ month (yuan)*	*Organizational contribution/ month (yuan)*	*Total amount/ month (yuan)*
Province-Level Positions (Tingji gan bu/廳級幹部)	800	800	1600
Bureau/Department-Level Head Positions (zhengchu/ju zhang/正處/局長)	700	700	1400
Bureau/Department-Level Deputy Positions (fuchu/fu ju zhang/副處/副局長)	600	600	1200
Deputy Inspectors (fu diaoyan yuan/副調研員)	550	550	1100
Section Chiefs (zhengkezhang/正科長)	450	450	900
Deputy Section Chiefs (fu kezhang/副科長)	375	375	750
Deputy Section Chiefs (fuzhuren keyuan/副主任科員)	300	300	600
Section Members (keyuan/科員)	200	200	400
Clerks (banshiyuan/辦事員)	150	150	300

Source: compiled by the author from interviews.

5.2.2 *Preparation of this innovation*

Fieldwork in this case study was conducted in September 2011 at the office of the municipal DIC of Jiangmen. Interviewees included but were not limited to municipal-level DIC, personnel management, fiscal, and propaganda departments, who were direct practitioners of the innovative policy and knew its decision process, at least their part in it. They worked jointly in designing the Integrity Pension Fund and turning it into reality. Collecting information from the interviewees enabled me to put the story pieces together and analyze the innovation's institutional constraints.

Policymakers from the Jiangmen Municipal DIC expressed two concerns about the fund's feasibility. The first was why civil servants would be allowed to

Table 5.4 Disciplinary sanctions and corresponding penalties, Jiangmen

Types of disciplinary sanctions for Party members	*Percentage of loss from the Fund*
Warnings (*jinggao chufen*)	50
Serious warnings (*yanzhong jinggao*)	70
Removal from internal Party positions (*chezhi*)	80
Party probation (*liudang chakan*)	90
Expulsion from the Party (*kaichu dangji*)	100

Source: compiled by the author from interviews.

take money back from the Integrity Pension Fund after five years. The second was the problem of currency devaluation, i.e., the fact that the money accumulated in the fund would be relatively reduced due to inflation. The Jiangmen DIC justified the proposed scheme as follows:

> *The median pay for all the civil servants was 750 per month. The reason we set five years as a cycle was based on the consideration that the newcomers to the civil servants get insufficient money with housing fund, and medical insurance was taken out from their salaries. Another consideration was the problem of currency devaluation; some people worried that the purchasing power of the fund would go down in a few years.*
>
> (LAI-2011-1)

Another policymaker from the municipal DIC added that it was unfair to view the Fund as an alternative way to increase government officials' salaries just because it involved money. The Fund was an essential "integrity investment," as he called it.

> *Some people mentioned it is the Fund of currency devaluation. However, it was also a worthwhile "Integrity Education Investment." This was a good example to solve the problem of the lack of input for integrity education and to solve the imbalance of input and output of such kind of education.*
>
> (LAI-2011-2)

An official from the Municipal Bureau of Finance declared that the public expenditure prepared for the Integrity Pension Fund was sufficient. His interview revealed that Jiangmen had allocated over 18 million for the Fund in 2010 alone. The fund received 2.2 billion in fiscal revenue for 2010 from Jiangmen City and an additional 0.4 billion from provincial fiscal transfer payments.

> *Jiangmen had achieved seven continuous years of a faster growth rate of revenue than the average level of Guangdong Province, so there was enough money to pay for the proposed Integrity Pension Fund. We could say that we were well prepared for the Fund to come from the perspective of the accumulated revenue.*
>
> (LAI-2011-3)

Most policymakers were heartbroken when the policy was terminated only three months after being implemented in July 2010, believing their efforts had been wasted. Their attempt to make an innovative policy that was, in their eyes, both positive and meaningful was denied by upper-level authorities and the public. One official from Jiangmen DIC expressed his opinion:

> *I felt so hurt. The Integrity Pension Fund was stopped just because of the media reports. In my opinion, if the fund accumulates to tens of thousands, anyone will consider the outcome before they tend to be corrupted. At least, the Pension Fund would make them think twice before [engaging in] corruption.*
>
> (LAI-2011-4)

A government official from the Municipal Bureau of Labor and Social Security did not agree with the critics online. He mentioned that the sudden termination of the Integrity Pension Fund heavily affected government officials' enthusiasm for joining the scheme. Responding to the key criticisms posed by the public, he made two points to debunk online claims that the Fund was an alternative way to enhance the welfare of government officials. First, the salary management system of government officials was implemented strictly according to relevant provisions. The Fund was not designed to raise their income levels, as salary management was strictly linked with local economic performance; to increase government officials' salaries, each municipal government had to achieve a minimum of 10% annual GDP growth. Though Jiangmen had met this threshold for many years, its civil servants' salaries did not grow as quickly as in other municipalities. Second, the Integrity Pension Fund was intended to build belief in integrity. Unlike previous integrity-building institutions, it stressed self-restriction over outside supervision, believing economic constraint would be more efficient than moral education (LAI-2011-5).

Policymakers emphasized their good policy intentions in interviews and media reports. According to their narratives, the Integrity Pension Fund was based on the following considerations. First, its combination of discipline and economic encouragement was an institutional innovation in the anti-corruption field and a valuable exploration of how new tools could combat corruption. It was an attempt to reform civil servants' salary management system and provide a potentially valuable lesson for other areas in China.

The second point was that this policy ensured government officials benefitted if they remained honest and suffered if they were corrupt. In the policymakers' eyes, if the long-term earnings were attractive enough, government officials might choose to maintain their integrity throughout their careers. On the other hand, if corrupt behavior were detected, the offending official faced deprivation via the Integrity Pension Fund, turning corrupt behavior from a "low-risk, high-profit" action to a "high-risk, low-profit" one. This might stop corruption at the psychological level, weakening the motivation for corruption and helping achieve the purpose of keeping government clean.

Third, this policy would help establish a culture of integrity. Corruption is the abuse of power at a superficial level; this policy led to a change of morals and inculcated the value of being a civil servant. As an economic mechanism, the Integrity Pension Fund restricted and stimulated government officials' integrity and educated them to become self-disciplined civil servants. This helped establish the psychological foundations for clean governance and created a culture of integrity. Thus, this policy was believed to provide support and backup for preventing and restraining corruption.

5.3 Institutional Voids of the Integrity Pension Fund

As mentioned in Chapter 4, the analytical framework of this study is institutional void. The following analytical part mainly discusses the case using data collected from interviews and media reports. Based on this information, I further analyze how the three kinds of support—organizational support, social support, and political support—interacted and contributed to the failure of the Jiangmen case.

5.3.1 *Organizational support*

The innovation involved a number of Party and government organs, including the Municipal DIC (市紀委), the Municipal Procuratorate (市檢察院), the Supervisory Bureau (市監察局), the Human Resource and Social Security Bureau (人力資源和社會保障局), the Fiscal Bureau (財政局), and the Propaganda Department of the Municipal Party Committee (市委宣傳部), requiring them to cooperate smoothly.

The municipal government of Jiangmen established a leading group (*lingdao xiaozu*/領導小組) to oversee the routine management of the funding pool, including designing the scheme and operating the Integrity Pension Fund daily. The leading group was housed in the municipal DIC and Supervision Bureau's building. The DIC of Jiangmen played a leading role in the innovation, presenting the scheme to the municipal Party Committee in July 2010 and securing its endorsement. The implementation process was then handed to the government departments.

The Municipal Human Resource Bureau and Social Security Bureau joined to help manage the proposed pension fund. They cooperated to affirm the number of civil servants who volunteered to participate in the fund. Jiangmen municipal government connected with correspondent banks to establish a separate account to collect and grant the fund. Another department involved was the Municipal Fiscal Bureau, from which the government's contributions to the fund came. As mentioned above, a Section Chief of the Municipal Fiscal Bureau suggested that the estimated fiscal expenditure for the Integrity Pension Fund was 18 million, adding that Jiangmen had enough financial support for the fund (LAI-2011-6). The Propaganda Bureau communicated with the media to publish articles on this topic and kept an eye on the public's reaction.

The government departments were ready for the innovation and got the Fund enacted in July 2010. All went well until harsh public criticism began flooding in.

5.3.2 *Social support*

Though organizational arrangements made the policy possible, the public had not bought into it. According to a report by *Southern Metropolis Daily* (*nan fang dushi bao*/南方都市報) on June 29, 2010, the policy provoked active social discussion. Comments on *Sina* (*xinlang weibo*) exploded a few days later, reaching more than 3,000 by July 2, 2010. The total comments on *Sina* and *Netease* (*wangyi*) reached 10,000. According to an official from the propaganda department of Jiangmen City, the main points the public expressed were as follows:

> *Netizens mainly questioned two points: the legitimacy of this policy with no approval from the National People's Congress of Jiangmen City; the second was*

that this policy could only prevent gentlemen from corruption, but not a villain (fang junzi bufang xiaoren/防君子不防小人). Furthermore, an online survey illustrated that 43.38% of the public disagreed with this innovative policy.

(LAI-2011-7)

Public opinion exerted pressure on the policy implementation. The public, represented by cyber citizens, pointed out that the so-called "innovative policy" had limitations. Essentially, it rewarded those who were not corrupt and combated corruption through monetary incentives; however, the public prioritized punishing corrupt government officials, not rewarding honest ones. According to media reports, netizens felt that rewarding ethical officials meant buying integrity, leading them to ask whether a similar fund should be established to reward members of the public for not committing a crime. The key to solving the problem of corruption, netizens believed, was to change the current environment. If tolerance for corruption remained unchanged, economic tools would not suffice to fight corruption. Fighting corruption with an economic tool, the public claimed, was like tempting cats with fish to encourage them to catch more mice. The problem was that, compared with the potential benefits of corruption, the Integrity Pension Fund was only a little fish. Without a systematic evaluation of their performance, would government officials give up the little fish of the Integrity Pension Fund for the bigger fish of corruption benefits, or perhaps even pursue both simultaneously?[14]

Online comments depicted the Integrity Pension Fund as "illegal, unscientific, unfair, and even immoral."[15] First, it was suspected that the Integrity Pension Fund was inconsistent with the Civil Service Law in PRC (*gongwuyuan fa*/公務員法), which did not support rewarding government officials. As an institution related to welfare, it contravened the Civil Service Law, which stated that "no department had any right to change civil servants' wage, welfare, and insurance policy by itself." Another point was that, before being sent to the individual's bank account, the government contributions to the Integrity Fund pool were public money deposited with individuals (*gongkuan sichun*/公款私存). A Jiangmen DIC official shared his reflections on the critics:

When public opinion became sharp, we held three seminars in Jiangmen and attended two in the provincial government. The former seminars got support from the municipal government of Jiangmen, while the latter seminars received harsh criticism from the provincial government.

(LAI-2011-8)

The second challenge was that the policy was not scientific and was not based on a careful investigation. The standard for depositing money into the fund pool was based on one's current executive level. For example, provincial-level deputies were required to deposit 1,600 yuan into the pool per month, and bureau-/department-level heads were required to deposit 1,400. However, a higher executive level by no means implied a greater potential for corruption; a department-level head with approval power had more opportunities to be corrupt than a provincial-level deputy with no administrative power or resources. As there was no evidentiary support for differentiating pool inputs by executive level, the public questioned the plan's reasonableness.

The third objection was that the scheme was unrealistic. Corrupt officials had one thing in common: they all believed they were lucky enough to escape punishment due to the imperfections in the investigation system. It was also doubtful whether the amount of money provided by the fund every five years could prevent thoughts of corruption from arising. The Integrity Pension Fund attempted anti-corruption reform by providing civil servants with high salaries (*gaoxin yanglian*/高薪養廉) but did not touch the root of corruption and so could hardly be effective.

Fourthly, the fund was even said to be immoral. The Integrity Pension Fund included personal money (from the individual's salary) and organizational money (public funds) to reward those who did not break laws and regulations with taxpayers' money. Since obeying laws and regulations and avoiding corruption were civil servants' fundamental obligations, why would they require additional rewards?

Online public opinion also pointed out that the "institutional innovation" tended to reward government officials while punishing the public by abusing the public expenditure portion of the Integrity Pension Fund; in effect, people holding administrative positions in the local government had designed a system that benefitted only them, which many deemed an "immoral" aspect of the fund.

Based on online criticisms, policymakers had many things to consider before enacting the scheme, such as establishing an evaluation system to investigate government officials' integrity performance. It was reasonable for the public to worry about government officials earning income by moonlighting while simultaneously getting fund payments. The second consideration was the region's unbalanced local development levels, as the fund's standards did not vary with each city's standard of living, weakening its ability to encourage government officials remain honest. Third, no single supervisory organ ensured the policy's effectiveness and was answerable for its enforcement. Corresponding policies were required to follow up on the Integrity Pension Fund and prevent people from receiving funds while engaging in corruption.

To the policymakers, the Integrity Pension Fund was an economic approach to combating corruption, which set it apart from traditional anti-corruption measures that mostly relied on moral appeals. As "anti-corruption by considerably increasing income," it was a positive effort in the anti-corruption battleground. The policy's positive aspect was that it directly addressed self-benefit and self-interest. Civil servants were viewed as ordinary people, not gods, and were expected to make mistakes. Based on this principle, the policy applied economic leverage to anti-corruption practices, encouraging government officials to restrain themselves and say no to temptations.

5.3.3 Political support

From the outset, the Integrity Pension Fund was endorsed and even encouraged by the CDIC, Guangdong DIC, and the Party Committee of Jiangmen. As a Municipal Party Committee Member of Jiangmen City stated:

> *It was noticeable that the CDIC even rewarded the policy design of the Integrity Pension Fund as the second prize of innovative policy at the national level.*
>
> (LAI-2011-9)

He held that the Integrity Pension Fund was a symbolic of Guangdong Province's political reforms. The fund got support from the then Party Secretary of Jiangmen, Chen Jixing, who wrote positive comments on "the Provisional Scheme of the Integrity Pension Fund in Jiangmen," noting it was worth making such an experiment.[16] Interestingly, no more related information from this official could be found online during my book writing.

The interviews showed that provincial support faded as social pressure grew, especially accusations that the Integrity Pension Fund was an attempt to increase civil servants' salaries by nearly 20 million yuan and criticisms that offering civil servants less money than they could earn from corruption would not keep them honest. A Municipal Party Committee Member of Jiangmen City recalled the details:

> *Three months after the operation of the fund, guidelines from the DIC of Guangdong came down that more research on this scheme needed to be carried out. In other words, we had to make clear the resource of funding, the standard of pay into the pool, and the policy of punishment before we let the scheme resume.*
>
> (LAI-2011-9)

Immediately after the challenges from social critics, the innovation lost the support of higher authorities, which turned out to be fatal. While the case started with sufficient political support from higher authorities, it quickly lost that support when faced with harsh social criticism. The DIC of Jiangmen terminated the fund in September 2010, only three months after it was implemented. Social support, as an intermediate factor, contributed to the innovation's failure, but what eventually determined its demise was the resulting loss of political support. Interestingly, social criticism was not seriously considered when designing future policies.

5.4 Conclusion

The policymakers' reflections on this event could be summarized as follows. The scheme's policymakers faced strong public criticism, mainly centering on why civil servants should be rewarded for remaining honest when it was their obligation to do so. The policymakers replied that establishing the Integrity Pension Fund was a positive attempt, given the current anti-corruption environment. Adopting economic tools into anti-corruption practice was a new idea for local DICs. The Fund was designed to raise the cost of criminality for government officials and dissuade them from becoming involved in corruption.

The public's second suspicion was whether this policy was an alternative way to enhance government officials' welfare, an accusation the DIC of Jiangmen denied. The DIC further explained that the Integrity Pension Fund had four features: duality, durability, risky nature, and constraints. Its first feature was duality, meaning that the scheme combined government expenditure and personal deposits instead of offering a direct economic subsidy from public funds. Secondly, it was durable, with withdrawal opportunities coming only every five years until retirement. Thirdly, it made it riskier for government officials to become involved in corruption, as any misbehavior would result in their losing all the money in the Fund, including the portion they had deposited. Lastly, it was constrained, acting as a warning, education, and supervision of government officials in the long run.

We find from the Jiangmen Case that, although an innovation may start with good intentions, it could fail because of insufficient institutional support, especially social support. Initially, the Integrity Pension Fund was supported politically by the provincial DIC and organizationally by related municipal-level departments, which worked together to design the policy in detail. However, the scheme encountered its greatest challenge from the public, whose growing criticism exposed the upper-level government to bottom-up pressure and led it to terminate the policy. Evidence illustrates how the three kinds of support jointly worked in the Jiangmen Case and led to the Integrity Pension Fund's final failure. Innovation without political blessing may not last long, even if it is well prepared.

Notes

1 Ranking and score of perception of corruption of Hong Kong by Transparency International: 2011: rank 12, score 8.4 (scoring from 0 to 10); 2012; rank 14, score 77; 2013: rank15, score 75; 2014: rank17, score 74; 2015: rank18, score 75; 2016: rank15, score 77

2 See http://finance.sina.com.cn/zl/international/20140613/101719403944.shtml Accessed on June 13, 2014.

3 Source: Hong Kong Bureau of Civil Service http://www.csb.gov.hk/tc_chi/admin/benefits/62.html. Accessed in December 2016.

4 See http://www.csb.gov.hk/tc_chi/admin/retirement/421.html. Accessed in November 2016.

5 See http://toutiao.baike.com/article-1312051.html An introduction of the Integrity Pension Fund in Hong Kong. Accessed in December 2016.

6 See http://www.time-weekly.com/html/20100707/9054_1.html. Jiangmen Integrity Pension Fund: anti-corruption or a raise of salary for civil servants? Accessed in September 2011.

7 See http://news.china.com/domestic/945/20131114/18146694.html Integrity Pension Fund in Liuyang. Accessed in November 2013.

8 Several municipal governments, Liuyang (in Hunan Province), Beijing, Tai'an (in Shandong Province), and Ankang (in Shaanxi Province), tried out this kind of integrity fund. They learned the experience of Hong Kong and Singapore, while the practical effectiveness remains to be tested.

9 GDP ranking of China cities in 2015: Guangdong Province has nine cities ranked in the top 100. January 21. Source: The National Bureau of Statistics http://news.dayoo.com/guangdong/201601/21/139996_46277409.htm. Accessed in November 2016.

10 *Wu Muluan*, How has China paid for civil servants over the past six decades? http://www.infzm.com/content/103619

11 The experiment of the Jiangmen Integrity Pension Fund terminated under great social pressure. *Guangzhou Evening Post* by Tian Enxiang, November 14, 2013.

12 Jiangmen plan to experiment with the Integrity Pension Fund from next month: the per capita annual subsidy of more than 4000, Guangzhou Evening Post, June 29, 2010 http://news.xinhuanet.com/politics/2010-06/29/c_12277847.htm

13 The experiment of the Jiangmen Integrity Pension Fund terminated under great social pressure. *Guangzhou Evening Post*, by Tian Enxiang, Accessed in November 2013. http://news.xinhuanet.com/legal/2013-11/13/c_125694504.htm

14 See Sichuan News, Cited from http://www.newssc.org/, Author: Ma Tianshuai

15 See http://star.news.sohu.com/20100630/n273176489.shtml, China Business Network, Author: Xuan Huahua, June 30, 2010

16 Jiangmen Integrity Pension Fund terminated within two months, *Southern Metropolis Daily*, http://news.ifeng.com/gundong/detail_2013_11/08/31063430_0.shtml Accessed in December 2013.

6 The Qianhai and Hengqin Cases

6.1 Anti-Corruption Agencies in China

This chapter analyzes a particular type of local anti-corruption innovation, i.e., anti-corruption agencies (ACA) reform. This kind of innovation contains features that usually take place at the grassroots level, are limited to a specific administrative area, and are hard to diffuse to other regions. Only a few regions have attempted to make innovations in ACA reform nationwide, all of which are in Guangdong Province—Qianhai, Hengqin, and Nansha (for the location of these regions, see Map 6.1).

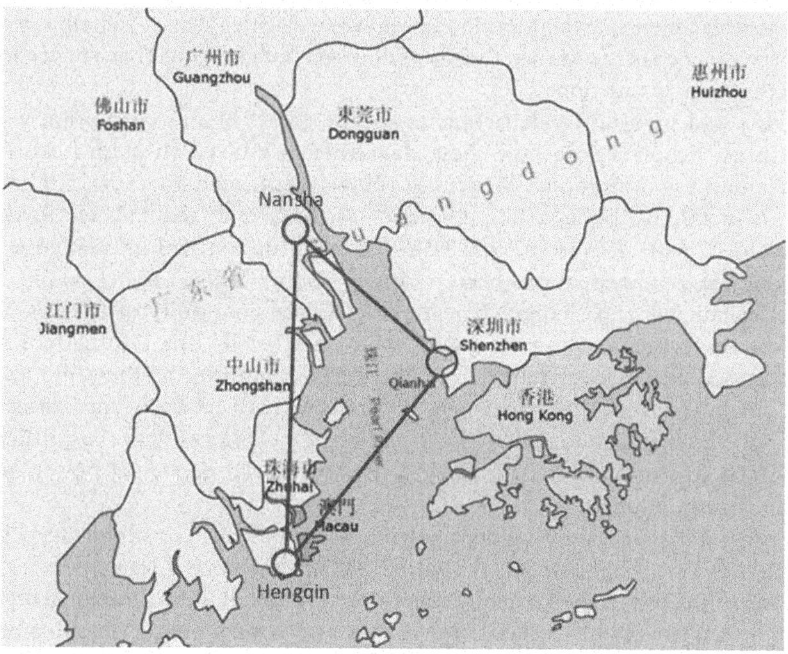

Map 6.1 Location of Qianhai (Shenzhen), Hengqin (Zhuhai), and Nansha (Guangzhou)

Source: Qianhai – the next growth engine for Guangdong and China, March 24, 2013, https://nothingtoworry1.wordpress.com/2013/03/24/qianhai-the-next-growth-engine-for-guangdong-and-china/

DOI: 10.4324/9781003112105-6

The Integrity Management Office of Hengqin (the IMO 横琴廉政辦公室) was established in September 2011. The office reset the function and relationship of anti-corruption government agencies by bringing four separate anti-corruption departments (the discipline inspection, supervision, procuratorate, and audit departments) into one. As separate departments, these four agencies functioned as stand-alone anti-corruption organs. Following the steps taken in Hengqin, the Qianhai Anti-corruption Bureau (the QAB 前海廉政管理局) was founded in May 2013. It contains three departments—investigation, corruption prevention, and community work. The departments' structure and function will be illustrated later in this chapter. Before getting into the Integrity Management Office's institutional merger, I must introduce the general information on anti-corruption-related government organs in China.

Each disciplinary inspection committee (DIC) is supervised by the Party Committee at the same level. As the principal organ to fight corruption, DICs at all levels check and examine Party members in administrative organs who implement the Party's guidelines and policies. DICs detect government officials who violate discipline or laws, handle complaints against government officials, and investigates accusations of illegal behaviors. Supervision departments supervise and inspect all civil servants, rather than merely Party cadres. Since 1993, supervision departments at the local level have worked with DICs at the same level. Supervision departments own the rights of inspection, investigation, suggestion, and disciplinary sanction.

DICs and supervision departments are the pillars of anti-corruption work in China. Scholars note how these departments evolved through historical and empirical limitations. Wedeman (2004) contended that the DIC system is ineffective because its jurisdiction is too loosely defined. He further concluded, with data from local DICs, that corruption had intensified even though the DIC system had been reformed. Gong (2008) further points out the dependency and change characteristics in the continuity of China's discipline inspection committee system. More specifically, the DIC system has limitations due to constraints from the Party committee at the same level. DIC members, including chiefs, are selected by the local Party committee at the same level and endorsed by the local People's Congress. It is thus difficult for DICs to supervise local leading cadres who hold personnel power over them (Gong, 2008).

Procuratorial and auditing departments also act as anti-corruption agencies. The Anti-corruption Bureau (*fantanju*/反貪局) was once a legal supervisory organ affiliated with the People's Procuratorial Office. It was a functional organ that investigates public officials for crimes and wrongdoing such as embezzlement, bribery, and duty crime. Now the anti-corruption bureau has been moved to DIC at the same level. Still, according to Chapter 8 of the Criminal Law, the procuratorial department's powers included initiating investigations of 12 kinds of criminality, including corruption, embezzlement, acquiring large amounts of property from unclear sources, sharing state-owned assets without permission, etc.

The last anti-corruption-related agency is the auditing department, whose core duty is to implement financial supervision and economic management at all levels of government. Local governments at or above the county level must establish audit departments with the power to investigate public affairs and obtain relevant testimonial material whenever needed, any relevant organization and concerned individual shall support and assist the auditing department and report the situation to the audit departments.

ACAs in China are fragmented into four departments and inevitably find it hard to cooperate, making it nearly impossible for them to investigate corruption effectively and independently. De Sousa (2010: 20) held that ACAs encounter various constraints to their mandate, which explains the meager results obtained by some of them. She further listed a series of factors for ACAs to achieve success. Some are internal to the agency (internal governance problems, weak leadership, and inadequacy or absence of management strategies), while others are external (lack of political will/support, unsustainable budgets, tense relationship with the public and the media in particular). Examining these factors to evaluate the current situation of ACAs in China may reveal an urgent need for their reform.

6.2 A Comparison of Two Cases

In this section, I present two cases in which reform of ACAs was attempted by reorganizing their structures, but with different results: the Qianhai Case and the Hengqin Case.

6.2.1 The Qianhai case

One of the innovations took place in Qianhai. Qianhai, more properly called the "Qianhai Shenzhen-Hong Kong Modern Service Cooperation Zone" (前海深港現代服務業合作區), is a special economic zone located on Shenzhen's Nanshan Peninsula, east of Lingdingyang, on the east coast of the Pearl River. Qianhai is the key point in the joint development of Guangzhou, Shenzhen, and Hong Kong. Its role is to enhance Shenzhen's, and even Guangdong Province's, cooperation with Hong Kong. Qianhai covers 15 square kilometers divided into three areas: Gui Wan, Qian Wan, and Ma Wan. It provides 650,000 jobs, with a resident population of 150,000 people.

In August 2010 (the 30th anniversary of the establishment of the Shenzhen Special Economic Zone), the state council formally approved the "Overall Development Plan of Qianhai Shenzhen-Hong Kong Modern Service Cooperation Zone" (前海深港現代化服務業合作區總體發展規劃), facilitating the set-up of a modern industrial zone in Qianhai. In March 2011, the plan was officially adopted into the "Twelfth Five-Year Plan" for national development. The decision to develop Qianhai special industrial zone marked the central government's ambitious intention to enhance China's market economy, as symbolized by Shenzhen.

Qianhai was designed to develop modern industry, service the close relationship between Hong Kong and mainland China, and pioneer industrial upgrading in the Pearl River Delta. Qianhai focuses on four pillar industries—finance, modern logistics, information services, and technology services—and other professional services.

Because of its unique position and dense settlement of enterprises, Qianhai also carries a high risk of corruption, establishing an independent institution to safeguard its development a priority. Thus, the ACA was established almost simultaneously with the building of Qianhai.

6.2.2 Qianhai Anti-corruption Bureau

The Qianhai Anti-corruption Bureau (*lianzheng jiandu ju/*廉政監督局, QAB) is subordinate to the municipal Party Committee and government of Shenzhen and is responsible for anti-corruption supervision in Qianhai. It reports to and is under the direct supervision of the Shenzhen municipal DIC. Unlike Hengqin, Qianhi avoids organizational difficulty by directly reporting to the municipal-level government.

In an interview, a deputy director of the QAB mentioned that the organizational change this innovation brought about, especially its investigation function, benefited the QAB, as the system design and joint task force of five separate bureaus facilitate its investigations. The QAB investigated 23 cases in 2014; both the quantity and quality were satisfactory to the QAB, according to Ye, a deputy director of QAB. The case workload almost equaled that of the Shenzhen municipal level investigations (LAI-2015-10).

The QAB's primary task is to investigate the government officials in charge of Qianhai's development, construction, operation, and management activities. The usual case investigation process is as follows. First, the Public Security Bureau (公安局) uses its many technical means and resources to gather useful information on a given case. The QAB can access a suspect's information within seconds, including their money transfer records, residence, travel records, and real estate purchasing records, through the police database and its internal network. After the background research is prepared, the QCA goes through different bureaus to approach different targets. If the case concerns CPC members, the QAB would ask the Commission for Discipline Inspection to have them to cooperate with the investigation. If the case involves citizens and business owners, the investigators would ask the police officer to bring the officials over for the prosecutor (who understands the law better) to question. At the same time, the audit bureau will be involved in opening a case against the suspect over economic issues. All of the above guarantee a surprisingly effective investigation (LAI-2015-10).

Reformers intended to make a structural change to the ACAs in Qianhai using independent ACAs like the ICAC as a model. However, it was difficult for them to do so in China's current political context as they had to deal with vested interests and complex power relationships among ACAs. The reformers started the experiment in a small area like the Qianhai New Area (a small administrative district of only 15 square kilometers), as it would be more likely to succeed than a municipal-level innovation. Another advantage of Qianhai was its small civil service, which made it easier for the ACA to carry out its investigation and supervision functions. All these conditions made Qianhai a suitable place to set up a new ACA. If the QAB were successful, it might be a good example of the efficacy of a joint anti-corruption task force. Whether the QAB model can be applied in a larger area is a different story.

The structure of the QAB imitates but is not the same as the ICAC. The ICAC model represents how an effective ACA changes the societal atmosphere with government and community support. Since its inception in 1974, the ICAC has embraced a three-pronged approach of law enforcement, prevention, and community education to fight corruption, helping make Hong Kong one of the least corrupt regions in the world. Learning from the ICAC's integrity management, the QAB set up three departments—investigation, corruption prevention, and community work—to enforce the Party's and State's political disciplines, investigate, punish, and prevent duty crime and economic crime, construct a corruption prevention system, conduct propaganda and education, etc. The QAB's administrative personnel are delegates of Shenzhen's municipal DIC, procuratorate, supervisory bureau, and auditing bureau. Shenzhen's municipal budget finances the QAB so that the independence of it is doubted.

6.2.3 The Hengqin case

Hengqin New District is located in south of Zhuhai and covers the whole of Hengqin Island (the largest of Zhuhai's 146 islands). It lies to the west of the Pearl River estuary, facing Macau and not far from Hong Kong. The Chinese government values Hengqin's commercially strategic location, calling it "a new bridge between Macao and the mainland." It faces the South China Sea to the south, is one kilometer from the Zhuhai Free Trade Zone to the north, links to the Modaomen Waterway (磨刀門水道) to the west, and is only 0.2 kilometers from Macau and 66 kilometers from Hong Kong in the east, making it the "One Nation, Two Systems" agreement's economic meeting point. As Hengqin is close to six airports—four international airports in Hong Kong, Macau, Guangzhou, and Shenzhen, and two domestic airports of Zhuhai and Foshan—it is a natural commercial hub connecting mainland China, Macau, and Hong Kong (see Map 6.2 as follows).

From an administrative perspective, Hengqin evolved from just a large Zhuhai island into a major development zone for Guangdong Province. Hengqin formed its township government in March 1989, affiliated with Xiangzhou district. From 1992 on, Hengqin Island was designed as one of three critical zones for

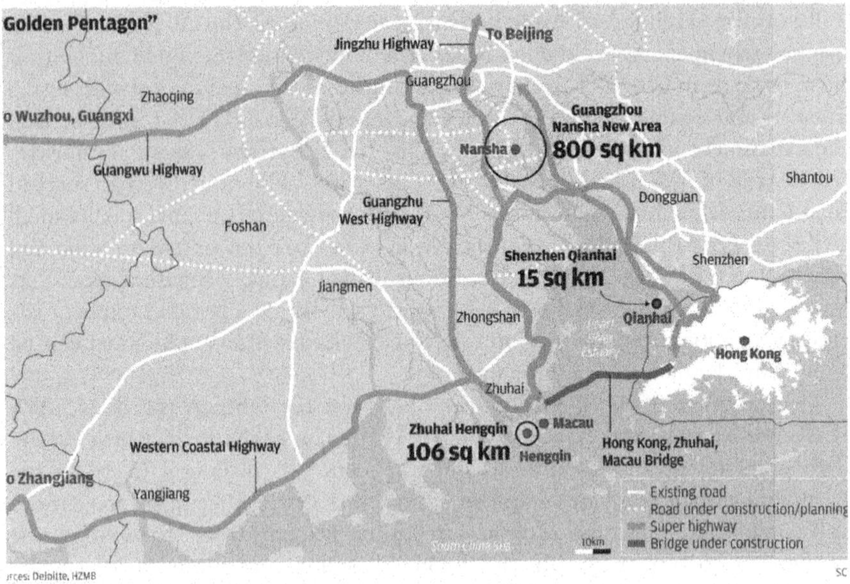

Map 6.2 Location of Hengqin in Greater Bay Area.

Source: Golden pentagon slowly taking shape, Denise Tsang, Published: 2 Sep, 2013, *South China Morning Post*, https://www.scmp.com/business/china-business/article/1301475/golden-pentagon-slowly-taking-shape

opening and developing Guangdong Province and functioned as a window opening Zhuhai to foreign investment. At the end of 1998, it was recognized as one of Zhuhai's five service areas.

There are four towns on Hengqin Island, including 11 villages with more than 7,500 people, of whom 4,203 are permanent residents of Hengqin Island. In August 2009, the State Council formally approved the implementation of Hengqin's overall development plan. Hengqin was brought into the Zhuhai special economic zone and designed to facilitate cooperation among Guangdong, Hong Kong, and Macau under the "One country, Two systems" policy. In December 2009, the Management Committee of Hengqin New Area was formally founded as a special economic zone of Guangdong Province and placed under the mandatory leadership of the Zhuhai municipal government. In March 2015, the Political Bureau of the CPC Central Committee approved Guangdong Province's Free Trade Area scheme, which included Hengqin.

6.2.4 *Integrity Management Office of Hengqin*

The Integrity Management Office (IMO) of Hengqin combines four departments—the Department of Comprehension (*zonghe chu*/綜合處), Department of Discipline Inspection and Supervision (*jijian jiancha chu*/紀檢監察處), Department of Audit and Supervision (*shenji jiandu chu*/審計監督處), and

Department of Communication and Negotiation (*diaocha lianluo chu/* 調查聯絡處)—into one body.

The Department of Comprehension runs the IMO's daily management work. It also organizes and coordinates corruption prevention work and is responsible for coordinating Party, government, factory, and village affairs. It takes charge of propaganda and education work to spread Party, administrative, financial, and economic discipline. The Department of Comprehension functions as a DIC to investigate Party members' misbehavior and evaluate administrative effectiveness. It carries out law enforcement supervisory work and is responsible for case management. The Department of Audit and Supervision conducts audit supervision on budgetary revenues and expenditures at the same levels. The Department of Communication contacts the procuratorial organs, transfers cases, and helps the procuratorial organs investigate duty crimes.

The Integrity Management Office of Hengqin has dual roles, serving as both an internal agency of the Hengqin government and a delegated institution of the upper-level government, Zhuhai. This means it is an internal department of the Hengqin New Area government functioning as an ACA with DIC, Supervision, Procuratorial Work, and Auditing departments working together. At the same time, it is also a dispatched agency of Zhuhai's municipal DIC, People's Procuratorate, Supervision Bureau, and Audit Bureau and must accept their professional guidance. Under China's current political arrangement, the Hengqin IMO follows the political leadership of Zhuhai Municipal CPC and Zhuhai DIC. Zhuhai Municipal DIC enjoys the power to appoint the Hengqin IMO director. The five bureaus mentioned above provide staff members for Hengqin's Integrity Office, which assigns them to different case operations and is responsible for their daily management. However, in important cases or work, the Hengqin Integrity Office answers to Zhuhai's Municipal DIC, Supervision Bureau, Auditing Bureau, and People's Procuratorate.

In a news article released three years after the establishment of the Hengqin Integrity Office, a vice-director of the Office confirmed the effectiveness of the IMO. He cited a widely reported bribery case in which a deputy section chief in the Hengqin New Area public construction bureau was arrested. Based on the previous procedure, the case would take several months to complete, from receiving initial clues to the final verification. However, the IMO concluded this case within only ten days, showing great efficiency (LAI-2014-11). As mentioned above, the Hengqin IMO intended to fight corruption by merging the functions of five bureaus into one body, accumulating rich lessons and experiences for future institutional innovations to learn from.

6.2.5 Two cases in comparison

The innovations broke the anti-corruption agencies' current structure. They explored building a unified department that combined DIC, public security, procuratorial work, audit, and supervision departments. The Hengqin and Qianhai cases were largely alike but had some differences. For example, the Qianhai case went more smoothly than the Hengqin case; Hengqin failed to integrate the Procuratorate into the IMO; and the Procuratorate assigned only two staff members to the job, not the whole department. There were no follow-up measures, so the project only went halfway. The QAB was the first agency to completely integrate the DIC, Supervisory Bureau, Procuratorate, Public Security Bureau, and Audit Office. The QAB had a clearer system than the Integrity Management Office of Hengqin, making it independent from other departments in Qianhai. Only with independence could the ACA function well in the long run. In this sense, the QAB achieved a better outcome than the IMO.

The Hengqin IMO's leaders knew this well. They realized that Qianhai was under the direct management of the Shenzhen City DIC, on behalf of its Municipal Party Committee and Municipal Government. Furthermore, Qianhai was merely an industrial zone instead of an administrative zone. This enabled it to run parallel with the Party Committee at the same level. Hengqin, con the other hand, could never claim to be parallel to the Party Committee. Here, "parallel" means the local DIC and the Party Committee at the same level shared equal power to make policy decisions. The DIC even has the power to check the Party Committee's behavior. The IMO is under the leadership of the Party Committee at the same level. The focus was on carrying out their work from the angle of the DIC of Hengqin. In the words of one policymaker, "I have not found out my position yet, not to say the parallel with Party committees." (LAI-2014-12)

The most vexing question Hengqin encountered was how to integrate these departments into one. The policymakers recognized that the journalists bragged about their experiences in newspapers; however, she was embarrassed to introduce the so-called "pioneering experiences" to outsiders so they could learn from them. She could only say, humbly, that they welcomed the exchange of ideas on this kind of innovation (LAI-2014-12) and were pleased to share their specific experience with others and to hear their comments and criticisms. She agreed that the innovation was well-intended and the former secretary of Guangdong DIC, Huang Xianyao, personally guided it from the beginning. After two years of reform, she realized its cost was nearly too much for their office to bear alone (LAI-2014-12).

The interviews clearly show that the Hengqin IMO's design was less satisfactory than the QAB's. I compare the two cases for several reasons. First, facing more difficulties, how could Hengqin find a way out of the current situation? A typical problem in this kind of innovation is integrating the procuratorate with other departments. If Hengqin could solve this problem, then the solution would be repeatable in other regions. Second, Hengqin covers a larger territory than Qianhai and deals with more administrative affairs related to residents, while Qianhai emphasizes commercial affairs to attract foreign investment, especially enterprises from Hong Kong. Based on this, both are cases for similar regions to imitate. Third, the significance of these two cases is obvious if one considers the larger picture. The Fourth Plenary Session of the 18th Central Committee of the CPC in 2014 mentioned the concept of "the rule of law," indicating that the Xi Jinping government's greatest priority in the coming decades was corruption-free government.

In the following analysis, I illustrate the process and difficulties the cases experienced and show how institutional support affects the innovations' fate.

6.3 Institutional Foundation

From a theoretical perspective, these innovations initially got enough social support but encountered difficulties getting organizational support. Things began positively in terms of political support but soon became more complicated. Together, these elements made it difficult to continue the innovation.

The essence of two globally recognized efficient anti-corruption agencies, the ICAC and the Corrupt Practices Investigation Bureau (CPIB), Singapore, is that they are both independent of the political system and have great autonomy. From the very start, the Integrity Office was viewed by mainstream media as a mainland China copy of the ICAC. A Xinhua Net report introduced the ICAC model and pointed out that the Hengqin model borrowed from the ICAC idea. Another report, from Caixin, recounted an integrity scholar's comment that the IMO experiment in Hengqin was less independent than the ICAC, a "halfway experiment" that was not thorough enough to function as the ICAC did due to a lack of upper-level government authorization. In the following part, I analyze the Qianhai and Hengqin cases from the perspectives of political, social, and organizational support.

6.3.1 Political support

The effectiveness that the QAB brought about does not mean that it encountered no difficulty. Although the QAB was established with high expectations from both municipal and provincial DICs, it has encountered dilemmas when operating in recent years.

The most prominent one is its lack of a legal basis. According to one QAB official, the establishment of the QAB hit the key elements of the current integrity management system, but did so at the risk of being illegal. The QAB's structure was quite different from the institutional settings of traditional management committees in inland provinces, which posed a serious problem: even though the QAB had merged these offices (departments/bureaus), it still lacked legal authority for the responsibilities it had assumed:

> *The DIC of Nanshan District in Shenzhen has the right to investigate any case and punish the corrupt officials within their administrative scope. The DIC of Nanshan District does not need to rely on any other agency to deal with the cases. However, the QAB is a dispatched agency of Shenzhen-DIC in Qianhai, and thus it is not an independent legal entity. The staffs are from five separate bureaus (the DIC, Supervisory Bureau, Procuratorate, Public Security Bureau, and Audit Office), and they have no legal enforcement power.*

> *Thus, it is a problem when they need to fulfill their job responsibilities. Moreover, the QAB as a dispatched agency of Shenzhen municipal government stationed in Qianhai is litigable. People have access to the court to sue the QAB for any of its misconduct. No court in China has the power to initiate a public prosecution against the DIC because of its obscure legal status. However, the QAB does not enjoy the same legal status as other local DICs do. This puts the QAB in a dangerous situation.*
>
> (LAI-2015-10)

Hengqin encountered another difficulty—changing attitudes among the higher-level DICs (Zhuhai City and Guangdong Province) as the situation evolved. Although interviewed officials from Zhuhai DIC asserted that higher-level DICs had triggered the innovation, they became less supportive when it encountered difficulties. The recent central government trend of trying new forms of supervision departments (i.e., merging DIC, procuratorate, and supervision departments) seemed to be good news for Hengqin and its innovations.

The Integrity Management Office obtained support from Guangdong DIC at the beginning of the innovation, especially from the secretary of Guangdong DIC, Huang Xianyao, who endorsed the idea of pioneering the innovation in mainland China. Huang Xianyao and Li Jia (then a member of the Standing Committee of the Guangdong Provincial Party Committee) attended the IMO's opening ceremony to show their support. As reported in the *Observer* (觀察者), Li stated that "Hengqin should carry on its innovation and learn from the successful experience of Hong Kong and Macau in combating corruption. We expect Hengqin to set an example for other areas in Zhuhai to create a corruption-free zone."

However, in practice, this innovation drew the interest of the procuratorate department and faced resistance. In an interview, an IMO policymaker noted that the then Party Secretary of Guangdong DIC was very supportive of the Hengqin innovation, reporting their efforts to Beijing shortly after the IMO's establishment. The Procurator-General of the Supreme People's Procuratorate became very anxious after seeing that report and ordered the IMO staff to stop the innovation or at least maintain the Procuratorate's independence at that level. From his standpoint, the IMO's establishment was unacceptable, as it meant the DIC had usurped the People's Procuratorate authority and made its functions merely symbolic. While Wang Qishan, the Secretary of the CDIC, had access to the report and was very supportive of the IMO, the conflicts did not stop there.

This example shows that even a peaceful lake can have significant undercurrents. While we could observe the IMO's opening ceremony, the underlying conflict of interest was harder to discern. According to interviews, officials from the Zhuhai Municipal DIC and the Party Committee of Zhuhai Municipal DIC expressed concerns about this innovation, noting that political reform is quite different from economic reform. Institutional innovation is a type of political reform and thus usually has difficulty succeeding. Economic reforms tend to have clear and measurable goals, such as increasing GDP, whereas political reforms' outcomes are hard to measure; even their goals are sometimes obscure.

Everyone has a unique understanding of how to implement political reform, making it hard to identify their outcomes. Moreover, bottom-up reforms are much more difficult to achieve than top-down. According to a standing member of the Party Committee of Zhuhai Municipal DIC, local initiatives are determined by China's power structure and decision-making process, and establishing the Hengqin Integrity Office illustrates the difficulty of political reform. It involved the power balance between Hengqin DIC and procuratorate and an endorsement from upper-level government, which together made the innovation complex and hard to implement (LAI-2014-13).

He further pointed out that both Zhuhai DIC and Hengqin DIC had prepared themselves well for the innovation. Common sense held that Hengqin, as a grassroots government, could hardly set a procuratorate department under its supervision. At the beginning of the innovation, central government inspection groups investigated the situation of Hengqin. The innovation also attracted other investigation organizations, including local DICs from across China. Some members of Zhuhai DIC, as the superior department of Hengqin DIC, were sent to Beijing to seek opinions from the CDIC and the Supreme Procuratorate. At that time, the central commissions almost all held that the Hengqin case ran the risk of being illegal.

The main concern for government officials from the Hengqin procuratorate department was *bianzhi* (the personnel levels allocated to an organization). When merged, the departments' *bianzhi* had to be transferred from the Hengqin procuratorate department to the new Hengqin Integrity Office. This affected the Supreme People's Procuratorate's bottom line, and it quickly recalled all civil servants belonging to public security organs, the procuratorate, and the court to their original units and forbade them to take external assignments.

Procuratorate departments held the right to sue and to handle cases; their authority and legitimacy would fade if these rights were assigned to the Integrity Office. This was the key point of dispute between the two departments. A Party Committee member of the Zhuhai DIC expressed that the law enforcement system was too complex to be simply merged into the Integrity Office, noting that even the management of a single cadre or an event involved several departments. The Hengqin model of Integrity Office failed to solve this problem under the current institutional setting as it was unclear which department was in charge, meaning many negotiations took place in many meetings (LAI-2014-13).

Another staff member of the Zhuhai DIC from BCP contended that there was little room for institutional innovation at local levels. Local officials often had a conservative attitude toward innovations. If a reform's direction was unclear or a new policy had yet to be announced by the central government, they would not take action; instead, they would wait for and follow the central government's next move. Local policymakers never started an "innovation" without a positive signal from above (LAI-2014-14).

The Bureau of Corruption Prevention (hereafter the BCP 預防腐敗局) in Zhuhai DIC issued the first Regulation on Corruption Prevention in China, and its officials were preparing a more detailed version when I interviewed them.

The regulation was an internal document prepared to gather ideas from the officials. Based on this regulation, policymakers would have to consider practical issues when formulating regulations instead of simply expecting the regulations to be perfect. According to one BCP official, a "perfect" regulation would not likely operate smoothly in real life, and the only way to make an innovation go smoothly was to consider all stakeholders' interests, as the Hengqin IMO did (LAI-2014-14).

Recent trends in China's top-level government made the innovation appear promising in the long run. The merging of several anti-corruption departments encouraged a structural change in ACAs in China. Experimental reforms of ACAs in Beijing, Shanxi, and Zhejiang were being carried out, providing an appropriate political atmosphere for the innovation, signaling that the Hengqin case should carry on, even make a breakthrough, and set an example.

6.3.2 Social support

Social support (i.e., support from social media and scholars) accompanied both cases throughout the innovative process. Social media gives a voice to the public, which expects the innovation to breathe fresh air into the fight against corruption. Scholars are a source of wisdom because they provide supportive comments and suggestions to perfect the policy design.

Right after the innovation of Hengqin was made public, it received much positive social feedback. Numerous newspaper articles called it mainland China's first attempt to reconstruct anti-corruption agencies and expected it to be an effective innovation to combat corruption. The reports, mainly from around September 2010, when the innovation was carried out, include articles in mainstream media outlets such as *Guangzhou Daily (廣州日報), Caixin (財新網), China News Service (中新社), and Observer (觀察者網).*

The Hengqin case was also expected to change anti-corruption agencies' functions: anti-corruption activity has been shifting from cooperation among several bureaus (where some casework was often slowed by red tape) to a better structured and more-united agency, meaning greater efficiency and a higher integrity management workload. Li Jia also intended to make the Hengqin Integrity Office a testing ground to check the effect of combining several bureaus into a single agency. In his words, the Hengqin Integrity Office was to become the CPU for the anti-corruption effort and a platform for information- and data-sharing cooperation with other government departments. The main innovation of the Hengqin Integrity Office is that it is a delegated agency answering to the upper-level Anti-corruption Bureau of Zhuhai Municipality.

Another form of social support was the voice of scholars. One scholar involved in the integrity study commented positively on the innovation, suggesting in a Caixin media report that the Hengqin case was a big step toward the horizontal integration of departments. "Horizontal integration," a concept he proposed, refers to integrating an anti-corruption system's relevant functional departments into one body, as Hengqin does. His other, more important concept, "longitudinal vertical reform," addresses agencies' lack of independence. According to him, Hengqin has made progress on horizontal integration, but empowerment by higher authorities is required for future enhancement. Zhuang Deshui, deputy director of the Research Center of Integrity Building (Peking University), commented on the Hengqin case from a design and development point of view, saying the Integrity Office of Hengqin had failed to set up an organizational form similar to the ICAC in Hong Kong and did include a close cooperation mechanism. As a result, it was equivalent to an integrated working team whose convenient working environment and conditions facilitate a collaborative mechanism; however, its staff are still under the leadership of relevant higher departments, and thus cannot be independent.

6.3.3 Organizational support

Organizational support is the area in which there is the largest difference between these two cases. The Hengqin innovation lacks organizational support and has put itself in a dangerous situation, while the Qianhai innovation has paved the way for organizational cooperation through institutional design. As mentioned above, the QAB was directly affiliated with the Municipal Party Committee of Shenzhen and the Shenzhen Municipal Government and drew its personnel from the municipal DIC, procuratorate, public security bureau, supervision, and audit office. Due to its direct dispatch from the municipal level, the QAB avoids organizational disputes because it does not answer to the same-level Party Committee. Furthermore, civil servants from the QAB's three departments (Investigation Department, Department of Corruption Prevention, and Department of Community Work) are co-equal, giving it a smoother foundation for organizational support than the Hengqin IMO.

Hengqin faces a major difficulty—the dispute over departmental interests—due to the reform's lack of a legal framework. As mentioned in the discussion on political support, the reason underlying the Hengqin case's difficulties is the dispute over departmental interests, an area in which the Hengqin Integrity Office must succeed if it is to move on. The first type of departmental interest dispute is the relationship between the Integrity Office and the Party Committee of Hengqin, making it difficult for the Integrity Office to fight against corruption.

> *What should also be clear is the actual position of the IMO within the integrity system of Hengqin. If the Office is regarded as an internal organization of the Party Committee of Hengqin, it cannot function and it was originally designed. We have to assign boundaries with the Party Committee at the same level and clarify our responsibilities with other departments.*
>
> (LAI-2014-12)

The IMO could hardly supervise the Party Committee of Hengqin. Though the Hengqin IMO is the Party Committee of Hengqin's watchdog and at the same level, the latter leads the former. This is the case for other DICs as well.

The relationship between DICs and Party Committees at the same level is subtle. The key to breaking the deadlock is to assure the independence of ACAs—in Hengqin's case, the IMO.

The second type is the dispute between the procuratorate department and the Integrity Office. One IMO policymaker noted that the first step in the innovation was to clarify the obligations of the IMO and the Party Committee. The next was to specify the work plan for conducting the innovation. She suggested that other departments might develop plans and bring them for further discussion. The IMO staff did not have a clear concept of how to make this innovation at that stage. Xu thought that other departments had to think about their functions under the new framework of the Integrity Office. As the procuratorate department has separated from the Integrity Office and returned to its original position, the IMO has had to think about its plan for routine jobs. However, its staff is certain that the innovation is moving in the right direction and is dedicated to keeping it going.

An official mentioned in the interview her concern about this problem:

> *We are confused about how to improve the function of the IMO with the given conditions. Now that the procuratorate department has already been separated from the Integrity Management Office, we believe that we are on the right track. We have to go forward instead of going backward. Now I am very distorted about the current situation of the office. If the position of our Integrity Office has been confirmed and gotten a wide reorganization, then my idea of this innovation would be clear, my work would be simple. By this I mean, now the position of the office is twisted and poses obstacles for our routine work.*
>
> (LAI-2014-12)

The staff members felt grievances about this. The secretary of Guangdong DIC made it clear at the Provincial Reform and Innovation Conference that the Hengqin Integrity Office could not be defined as an internal agency, as it follows what upper-level government says. However, in reality, this was not the case.

The dilemma was that the innovation took the risk of breaking the Constitution of the PRC, which makes it clear that the procuratorate department exercises procuratorial authority independently and is not subject to interference by administrative organs, social organizations, and individuals. This established principle allows the procuratorate department to function well. The biggest risk of this innovation was the IMO's attempt to assume leadership over the procuratorate department, challenging the Constitution and the procuratorate's independence.

The reformers sought legal support for their innovation. They had to answer questions from the procuratorial department about having them as a part of the IMO and under its supervision. The solution to this problem depended on two considerations. The first was how to rationalize the founding of the Integrity Office. Some higher-level government leaders lack legal awareness and have not put the legitimacy of the Integrity Office on their agenda. It was essential to find legal support if the innovation were to survive the procuratorate department's challenge and continue. The second consideration was how to remove future obstacles to the innovation and thus set an example for related innovations. With the legal risk unresolved, it was nearly impossible for the innovation to be diffused to other local areas. However, legal support cannot be easily achieved from the bottom; it usually flows from the top down.

What the Integrity Office can do at the moment is enhance resource and information sharing. Since the procuratorate department has been separated from the IMO, the innovation must await other opportunities and prepare to embrace the procuratorate department again someday.

6.4 Conclusion

The common features of the two cases can be summarized as follows. Both cases are experiments in innovative ACA reform at local levels that enjoy political and social support. Where they differ is in the extent of their organizational support. Without a reasonable institutional design, disputes among departments would complicate things.

We can draw some conclusions from the Hengqin case. It symbolizes a typical kind of anti-corruption innovation, the reform of ACAs. It sets an example for other cases to carry on, though it is not perfect. Overall, the Hengqin Case is continuing despite its difficulties. At the end of 2013, Hengqin formally restored the People's Procuratorate and the Court, conceding that that part of the innovation had failed, costing the Hengqin IMO part of the Integrity Office's procuratorial functions. The innovation received sufficient social support from the public, media, and scholars. Social actors welcomed the innovation, believing it necessary for the enhancement of ACAs in China. Regarding practical suggestions, scholars stressed that the innovation's priority should be to award more authority to local levels, as greater ACA independence makes success in the battle against corruption more likely.

The IMO's political support began strong but weakened afterwards. The provincial DIC initially endorsed the IMO, but challenges from the central-level procuratorate department made the municipal DIC hesitate to support the innovation further.

The innovation is not yet successful due to a fatal lack of organizational support, mainly stemming from two instances of organizational resistance—the withdrawal of the Party Committee of Hengqin, and the procuratorate department's disagreement with the decision to place it under the IMO. The cause for both difficulties was the IMO's lack of legal basis. The Hengqin IMO's best way forward is to await a future opportunity to become an independent, legal ACA.

While the innovation's initial plan was to obtain some "independence" from the Party Committee at the same level, there is no denying that the IMO is subject to multiple levels of leadership from above. Thus, its fate is, to some extent, in the hands of upper-level authorities. It also must solve the problem of its chief manager's bureaucratic despotism, which makes the innovation unstable.

Furthermore, getting a legal license from higher-level departments would be desirable. One cadre from Zhuhai's procuratorial system said that if the Integrity Office wanted to learn from the ICAC of Hong Kong, it had to re-equip its organizational structure and rebuild its operational process to fight corruption more effectively. However, the current separation of procuratorial functions is unlikely to change soon.

So far, there have been no clear instructions from Guangdong Provincial DIC ordering the Hengqin Integrity Office and QAB to replicate their innovation. The Guangdong Provincial DIC only proposes that the local government should provide a free and easy environment for the Hengqin Integrity Office and the QAB, so both can provide fresh experiences for a future anti-corruption campaign in Guangdong Province. How the Hengqin Integrity Office and QAB will perform in the future and what the Central DIC's next step will be need further observation. The signal from the central level to build a unified national ACA brings the idea of independent ACAs to the local level. Again, political support fosters local innovations.

7 The Shenzhen Case

In recent years, the central government realized the urgency and necessity of reforming "three public expenditures"—i.e., government officials' business trips, purchasing and operating government vehicles, and government hospitality activities. In 2012, these three public expenditures accounted for 10% of China's annual revenues,[1] a large amount compared to other countries. The growing public expenditure causes significant financial losses and severely damages the government's public image. The central government enacted the Eight Rules against extravagant spending of public money in December 2012 and demonstrated a strong political will to restrict extravagance.[2]

7.1 Extravagant Expenditure on Government Vehicles

The expenditure on government vehicles accounts for the largest amount of the three public expenditures, which has become increasingly extravagant and caused broad public criticism. The reform, which aims to reduce the abuse of government vehicles to save public expenditure, can be traced back to 2008, when the 11th National Committee Meeting of Chinese People's Political Consultative Conference (CPPCC) was held. At that meeting, one of the eight Democratic Parties (*min zhu dang pai*/民主黨派) in China, the Revolutionary Committee of the Chinese Kuomintang (RCCK, *min zhu ge ming dang*/民主革命黨) proposed reforming expenditures on government vehicles all over China.[3] As one of the Democratic Parties of China, RCCK participates in state affairs by lending a hand on administrative issues and policy consulting. RCCK listed four points to support the necessity and urgency of this course of action. First, government vehicle costs were high, creating a heavy financial burden. The annual operating cost for a government vehicle (including the driver's salary and welfare) was at least 60,000 yuan and sometimes over 100,000 yuan, accounting for 6% to 12% of annual fiscal expenditures. Second, the private use of government vehicles is common. Third, overstretching and equipping vehicles above standard continues despite repeated prohibitions. Fourth, the efficiency of government vehicles is low and a huge source of waste. Not including public institutions (e.g., state-owned enterprises, the military, hospitals, schools, and others), China has over 200 million government vehicles costing 150 to 200 billion yuan annually, a

DOI: 10.4324/9781003112105-7

lavish expenditure that has been described as "corruption on wheels" (*che lun shang de fu bai*/車輪上的腐敗).

As reported by Netease, one of the most influential web portals in China with the largest number of users,[4] expenditures on government vehicles accounted for over 60% of the three expenditures in recent years.[5] The data were collected and sorted by "The Scheme for government vehicle reform at the central level" (*zhongyang he guojia jiguan gongwu yongche zhidu gaige fang'an*). Netease's figures indicate that the three public expenditures declined from 9.364 billion to 7.151 billion from 2011 to 2014, with government vehicles accounting for 5.915 billion, 44.32 billion, 43.99 billion, and 41.27 billion of that in each of the four years, respectively. These data support the central government's government vehicle reform plan.

7.2 The Reform of Government Vehicles

The official term "government vehicle" initially appeared in the quotas and standards for government vehicles in central state organs (*zhongyang guojia jiguan gongwu yongche bianzhi he peibei biaozhun de guiding*/中央國家機關公務用車編制和配備標準的規定) in 2004.

In July 2014, the central government announced "the Comprehensive Guide to Push Forward the Reform of Government Vehicle Management" (*guanyu quanmian tuijin gongwu yongche zhidu gaige de zhidao yijian*, hereafter "The Guide"), at which time central government agencies began reforming the management of government vehicles. The Guide emphasized the significance of this reform: since the founding of the PRC, government vehicle service was supplied in the form of vehicles and corresponding services to guarantee civil servants' business trips. However, the traditional role of government vehicles does not suit the transition to a socialist economy. The government has long been criticized for owning too many vehicles, leading to excessive operating costs. For example, according to a survey reported by *China Times* (華夏時報), the Party and government organs at all levels owned more than 2 million government vehicles, at an annual cost of at least 60,000 yuan each. It was estimated that the government spent 150 to 200 billion yuan annually to operate and maintain government vehicles, accounting for 6% to 12% of total government expenditures.[6]

The intensive use of government vehicles has some side effects, including contributing to air pollution in Beijing and other major cities.[7] The frequently observed private use of government vehicles further raised pubic concerns. To solve these problems and react to public critics, top leaders of the central government decided to reform the management of government vehicles nationwide. In recent years, local governments and agencies explored this reform and gained experience dealing with government vehicle abuse.

Another guiding document, named "The Scheme for government vehicle reform at the central level" (*zhongyang he guojia jiguan gongwu yongche zhidu gaige fang'an*), was officially published at the same time to guide local governments and signal the start of China's reform of government vehicles. Per the 2014 central scheme, central and local governments were to stop using general government vehicles, encourage civil servants to use public transportation, and pay appropriate subsidies for daily transportation. Notable, the two documents show a roadmap for the reform and set a clear timeline for local-level reforms. Nationwide, governmental agencies were encouraged to complete the reform before the end of 2015. A report from *Netease* clarifies the government vehicles involved in the reform[8] and shows the overall scope of the central-level reform conducted in 2014. The scheme abolished two kinds of government vehicles: government vehicles for cadres at or below the deputy ministerial level and all general government vehicles for central departments. Two kinds of government vehicles remained after the reform: those for emergency use and those for technical tasks. Local governments took various measures following the central guidance. The detailed process is presented in the following section.

7.3 Government Vehicle Reform at Local Levels

The Guide required all provinces and directly supervised municipalities to establish leading groups for the reform and asked local governments to design reform schemes based on local conditions. All provincial-level reform schemes were to be submitted to the central leading group and endorsed before local governments put them into practice.

Based on The Guide, the deadline for local levels to complete the reform was the end of 2015. One year after the Guide was published, the deputy director of the National Development and Reform Commission (NDRC, *guojia fazhan gaige weiyuanhui*) reported that 20 provinces had submitted their reform schemes, 16 of which[9] had been authorized by the central leading group,[10] which was affiliated to NDRC. Eventually, by the end of 2015, all provincial-level reform schemes were approved.[11]

According to an official of the central leading group in charge of the government vehicle reform, the central government adopted a supportive attitude towards local governments' reform measures. There were, however, concerns, the first being regional disparity. China has great regional disparities and differences at various government levels. The reason the central government only published a rough guide instead of a specific scheme for local governments was to allow local governments to make suitable schemes based on local realities.

The official also expressed the central government's expectation for the effectiveness of this reform—to reduce the expenditures on wheels after the reform. He introduced data proving that the reform outcomes expected at the central level were "beyond expectations." While the plan estimated annual savings of around 7%, even after expenditures on subsidies were included, that actual reduction in expenditures at the central level was 10.75%, and 7.88% on average in the 16 provinces.[12] The provinces that implemented schemes approved by the central leading group could be seen as pioneers of local-level government vehicle reform.[13]

The reform of government vehicle management is now spreading across the country. Local governments have tried three different modes of government vehicle reform: the "monetization approach" (貨幣方式), a subsidy paid to government officials (as practiced in Shenzhen and Huizhou); the "management approach" (管理方式), which refers to establishing an agency to manage all government vehicles (as practiced in Kunming); and the "semi-monetization approach" (半貨幣方式), which combines the first two models by outsourcing government vehicle management and providing a partial subsidy for transportation costs (as practiced in Hangzhou). These three modes have their own characteristics and show the wisdom of choosing an approach that fits local conditions.[14]

The current central policy follows the third model, the "semi-monetization approach." The central leading group for this reform abolished general government vehicles and provided a certain subsidy to civil servants based on their administrative levels. Local governments are now introducing local policies that fit their situations. Guangdong Province also adopted the third mode. When asked why, the deputy director of the public prosecutors' office of Guangdong Province, Xie Guliang, explained that it fit Guangdong's situation and was a "win-win" choice for government officials and the public sector. Guangdong's car ownership rate is 20–30 households per hundred vehicles, meaning the reform is less likely to inconvenience public officials' daily transport than in other localities. The "monetization approach" reduced the government's financial burden and solved the problem of abuse of government vehicles.[15]

7.3.1 Reform in Guangdong and Shenzhen

In 1993, Guangdong became the first province to reform government vehicle management. Specifically, the reform was initiated by the town of Shatian in Dongguan City. It terminated government vehicle use and paid a transportation subsidy to civil servants, resulting in a 54% drop in expenditures on government vehicles. This kind of reform started from local voluntary efforts and then diffused to other counties and cities in Guangdong. Ten years later, in 2003, the provincial DIC enacted the Suggestion to Push the Reform of Government Vehicle Management (*guanyu jiji wentuo tuijin gongwu yongche zhidu gaige de yijian*). The Suggestion symbolized approval and guidelines from the provincial authority.[16]

Shenzhen was the second city to voluntarily propose a scheme to reform the management of government vehicles, doing so right before the central government introduced the Guide in July 2014. Shenzhen is known for offering its government officials salaries and welfare benefits higher than in most cities in China. Those required to give back government vehicles received financial subsidies in compensation. The reform has become a controversial topic. Citizens call the subsidies unnecessary extra income for government officials, while the officials themselves are unhappy they can no longer use government vehicles as they like.

It took 20 years to realize the reform of government vehicles in Shenzhen, and the process this innovation followed can best be described as a "zig-zag." The timeline of the reform was as follows (based on a media report):

I summarize several key points in Table 7.1. The timeline for the reform is more than twenty years until it ultimately comes to fruition in 2014. During the two decades, the idea of conducting this reform met obstacles and was almost

Table 7.1 The timeline of the government vehicle reform in Shenzhen

Time	*Key issues about the reform*	*The public sector involved*
1994	The idea to reform use of government vehicles was proposed by Liang Wensen, a member of the municipal People's Consultative Conference (*zhengxie*) of Shenzhen. The name of the proposal was "the control of government vehicles in administrative departments and state-owned enterprises." This is the first voice heard from the public about reform of government vehicles in Shenzhen.	The People's Consultative Conference of Shenzhen
2003	On the fifth session of the Third People's Conference of Shenzhen, the municipal people's representative, Zheng Xueding, and others jointly adopted a proposal to urge the municipal government to speed up the pace of the reform on government vehicles.	The People's Congress of Shenzhen
2003	The municipal office of institutions and reform set up a research group for government vehicle reform and reported a preliminary scheme.	The municipal office of institutions and reform
2004	The municipal government set up the leading group and office for government vehicle reform.	The municipal government of Shenzhen
2007	On the third session of the Fourth People's Conference of Shenzhen, Zheng Xueding's scheme got a reply from the municipal Department of Development and Reform, which stated that it was not the suitable time to conduct the Shenzhen government vehicle reform, since it was not good timing and conditions were not mature enough.	The municipal Department of Development and Reform
2011	The return of Shenzhen Reform Office. In August 2011, an expert reform panel was held. Zhang Siping, a municipal committee member, indicated that the scheme of government vehicle reform had already been activated.	Shenzhen Reform Office
2012	Shenzhen municipal government for the first time opened up to the public about "three expenditures." Among which, bus purchase and operating cost in 2011 accounted for 74.88% of all "three expenditures."	Shenzhen municipal government
2013	Deputy secretary general of the Shenzhen municipal Party committee, director of the municipal reform office, Le Zheng said that Shenzhen government vehicle reform was in the making, and was expected to be formally launched in 2014.	Shenzhen Reform Office

(*Continued*)

Table 7.1 The timeline of the government vehicle reform in Shenzhen (*Continued*)

Time	*Key issues about the reform*	*The public sector involved*
January 19, 2014	Director of the Municipal People's Congress standing committee of Shenzhen, Bai Tian, revealed that the reform scheme had been formed.	Municipal People's Congress standing committee of Shenzhen
January 21, 2014	*Southern metropolis daily news* in Shenzhen calls for curbing the private use of government vehicles. It urges to further standardize the government vehicle management and start the Shenzhen reform as soon as possible.	*Southern metropolis daily news*
January 28, 2014	The Mayor of Shenzhen, Xu Qin, answered the questions from journalists about the reform. He said, "I hope the scheme will be acceptable to both the public and civil servants."	Mayor of Shenzhen
March 2014	Shenzhen scheme of government vehicle reform was published.	The leading group of the reform, Shenzhen
2015	Detailed version of the Shenzhen scheme was sent to the district level and was implemented.	The leading group of the reform at district level

Note: Compiled by the author from a media report about policies on reform of government vehicles made by Fenghuang web.[17]

given up at a time. Media reports (Fenghuang web) that some offices related to this reform were set up, revoked, and then recovered, indicating the obstacles to the reform are large and touch upon the interests of government officials.

The second point is that the reform included a number of the government institutions involved, including but not limited to the People's Consultative Conference of Shenzhen, the People's Congress of Shenzhen, the municipal government of Shenzhen, the municipal Department of Development and Reform, and leading reform groups at all levels. With so many departments working on the reform jointly, close collaboration in policy design and implementation would be required. Many negotiations and discussions will be necessary before a consensus can be reached on the scheme.

Third, the launch of the central-level reform accelerated the pace of this reform. Though Shenzhen has been one of the leading reform pioneers at the national level, it has encountered difficulties with the democratic system. For an extended period, the idea of this reform could not be pushed forward, and even went backward. It reminds us that gaining the endorsement and encouragement of higher-level governments is necessary if local levels are to do what they now think of but once feared.

It is interesting to observe the resistance policy designers encountered in making innovative policies. Shenzhen municipal government met some difficulties when they designed and implemented the policy. For example, the amount of subsidy was a debatable issue; the level of civil servants allowed to own official vehicles was yet to be decided; and taking government vehicles back from those who had them was difficult. I interviewed insiders about how the reform overcame these difficulties.

Accordingly, there were also dynamics in favor of Shenzhen making this reform happen. As a pioneer of economic and political reforms among coastal cities, Shenzhen has been applying innovative methods to enhance local development and governance. The interviewee, a clerk of the Pingshan Reform Office, stated when I asked about the motivation of this reform that Shenzhen had more political awareness than inland cities. He stressed that coastal cities usually made the first move in institutional innovations. Cities such as Shenzhen, Guangzhou, and Shanghai have better economic performance, which lays a foundation for their pursuit of political reform.

> *Policies from the central government usually take different forms at local levels. Coastal cities like Guangzhou, Shenzhen, and Shanghai strictly follow policies from the upper levels. However, you may find that in inland cities, many county-level government buildings are built as luxuriously as the White House. However, this will never happen in Shenzhen. Local officials of inland cities would take the advantage of their political power for self-benefit. It is not the same case in Shenzhen.*
>
> (LAI-2015-15)

As a pioneer in making innovations, Shenzhen devised the Scheme to Reform the Management of the Municipal Government Vehicles (深圳市直機關公務車改革實施方案) in March 2014, mere months before the central government's similar move, targeting only those government officials at or below the bureau level. For example, the Party Secretary of a district in Shenzhen was excluded because he held a department-level position (above the bureau level). The scheme set practical steps for the reform, including that it should be implemented in municipal departments first and then spread to procuratorial organs and people's courts. It also suggested government vehicles should all be collected, with some being returned to departments in real need (based on the regulations) and the rest going to public auction. Monthly subsidies would be paid to the affected government officials based on their bureaucratic level, though the amount of the subsidies was not publicized.[18] While the scheme only an outline, it generated some ideas about the reform. I conducted interviews in a district of Shenzhen, Pingshan District, to learn more about the scheme's implementation.

7.3.2 The Pingshan case

Before getting into the case, I shall introduce Pingshan's location, population, and economic situation in Shenzhen to explain why it was chosen as the location for my case. Pingshan District, set up in June 2009 and located in the northeast part of Shenzhen, is one of four new districts (Guangming, Longhua, Pingshan, and Dapeng) of Shenzhen. The total area of Pingshan District is 166 square kilometers, and its population has reached 0.6 million (of whom 0.36 million are registered). Pingshan's annual GDP was 42.399 billion yuan in 2015. Pingshan District is about 30 kilometers from such downtown areas as the Luohu and Futian districts. Neighboring Dongguan and Huizhou, it is an important channel to eastern Guangdong and plays a key role in the strategy for developing "great industries, great petrochemicals, great logistics and great supporting facilities" on the eastern coast of the Pearl River Mouth. Pingshan is home to over 2,000 enterprises, including 10 Fortune 500 companies.

I chose Pingshan as my case to illustrate the government vehicle reform for several reasons. First, its leaders established reform and innovation as the basis for the district's future development. The founding of Pingshan District symbolizes Shenzhen's spirit of reform. After five years of efforts, Pingshan has undertaken five national-level and six municipal-level reform programs and has gradually explored the so-called "Pingshan mode" as a representative district pioneer in the reform and innovation area.[19] A media report from the *South China Daily* expressed that Pingshan carried the "reform gene"[20] from the outset, piloting various innovative regional, provincial, and even national policies.

Second, as a relatively remote district, Pingshan had the greatest motivation to push government vehicle reform and get a larger subsidy, although the outcome was that it received an equal amount of subsidy from the reform. Most of its government officials live in the downtown area of Shenzhen and it takes them three to four hours to shuttle between their home and Pingshan. Before the reform, some government vehicles were used as shuttle buses and provided services for government officials; since the reform, the district government has booked services from social buses, thereby saving resources.[21]

The third reason is convenience. Since I know some civil servants in Pingshan, I could conduct in-depth interviews and make detailed observations. They shared their views on this issue and provided sufficient material about the reform. In addition to individual interviews, I also conducted a focus group interview in which the civil servants discussed and debated the reform. Through the collection of first-hand data, the picture of the innovation became complete, with a wide range of voices heard.

My target interviewees were mainly officials involved in policymaking and implementation and those affected by the particular policy innovation. They were civil servants from the Reform Office (改革辦公室), the Investigation Section (調研科), the DIC of Pingshan (坪山紀委), and the Wisdom Social Service Center (智慧社會服務中心) who had either participated in or had personal experience of the policymaking process. They were willing to share their opinions about the innovation, and I was ready to listen to all sorts of ideas from them. I explored each person's attitude toward the reform and found some thoughts that would never appear on a public occasion, helping reveal the complexity of the reform from a micro perspective. How did the individuals behave in the policymaking and policy implementation processes? What were their reactions to the reform's outcome? Different opinions clashed, and the story became increasingly interesting.

In the following part, I discuss and analyze this case from the institutional void theoretical framework, as in the last three cases. Again, the case is illustrated from three perspectives—political, organizational, and social support—to map how the reform was designed, implemented, and succeeded. Some lessons can be learned from comparisons with the previous three cases.

7.4 Institutional Foundation

This innovation was supported by upper-level government, the departments involved, and the general public. Analyzing the case of Pingshan illustrated the entire innovation process, revealing its origins, its support from Shenzhen's leading group in charge of government vehicle reform, its drawbacks and how reformers overcame them, and its smooth implementation since March 2014. This does not mean the innovation met no difficulties; however, it had a solid institutional foundation to conquer them.

7.4.1 Political support

There is no denying that the reform got support from the central government's decision to reform government vehicles before the end of 2014, symbolizing its support for local-level reforms on government vehicles. Second, and more practically, the 2014 central reform scheme set an example for local governments to follow. The Guide clarified that the central government intended to make a cleaner government and fight "waste on wheels of government vehicles," transform government functions, and advance logistical services, thereby enhancing the government's image in response to public criticisms. The Guide further urged local-level governments to realize the reform's significance and take action as soon as possible.[22]

Like the central government, local governments established leading groups for the reform at corresponding levels. However, the leading groups took various forms instead of only answering to the NDRC as the central level did. Some were affiliated with the Development and Reform Commission (*fagaiwei*/發改委); some reported to local DICs; and others may have been led by Government Offices such as the Reform Office.[23] This phenomenon supports the idea that local-level reform has unique characteristics and shows that local governments have the flexibility and autonomy to choose different reform strategies based on local conditions.

It was an institutional innovation, though the central-level government had already published the 2014 scheme. As mentioned in the previous introduction, the government vehicle reform in Shenzhen can be traced back 20 years. Shenzhen decided to reform government vehicles on its own, not as a political task received from upper-level governments. An interviewee from the leading reform group in Pingshan told me how Shenzhen made the innovation from his point of view:

> *There is a very limited experience to learn from at the very beginning of the reform since Shenzhen got down to doing this quite early, earlier than most other cities. When the scheme came out finally in 2014, we had no step-by-step guideline for how to implement the scheme and make the reform happen. The municipal-level leading group only offered us a direction to follow. We rely on ourselves at most times.*
>
> (LAI-2015-15)

Based on this interviewee's statement, the ideas for both the reform and the scheme's implementation depended on Shenzhen and its districts, though little local experience could be seen in early 2014. In this view, Shenzhen reform was a local innovation, not an imitation of what the upper-level government was doing.

As stated above, Shenzhen has supported this reform since 2013 and has undoubtedly encountered related difficulties over the past two decades. Ten districts of Shenzhen established leading groups for the reform.[24] At the early stage of the reform, members of the leading groups sat together and discussed the proposed schemes every two weeks. A member of the leading group of Pingshan recalled in the interview that Shenzhen supported Pingshan's reform and even assigned Pingshan to be one of the experimental districts of the reform:

> *The leading groups of Pingshan District and Futian District were required by the leading municipal group to draft a scheme respectively and submit it to the municipal level. The leading group of Shenzhen considers the different distances for ten districts to reach the municipal government. They selected Pingshan and Futian as representative cases for both remote and close districts. We also interpret it as a signal of the superior level's trust towards Pingshan's ability to design an innovative policy.*
>
> (LAI-2015-16)

Shenzhen municipal government supported the innovation at the district level in two ways. One was to provide model schemes for other districts to imitate. The leading group at the municipal level set accurate standards for the reform, giving local reformers an example to follow. In this way, local innovations ran far fewer political risks than they would have without such guidance. The other way was to keep in touch with local reformers through regular meetings where district-level difficulties could be opened for discussion and inquiry. Some were common difficulties; others were unique. For example, the outskirt districts proposed to set the subsidies to civil servants higher than those in urban areas, while the leading group rejected the proposal in the name of the central government's guidance that all regions should share the same amount of subsidies. The political support from the higher-level government could be summarized as setting principles for the lower levels and keeping them on track.

The government vehicles in Shenzhen now all carry a "government vehicle" logo to show that they are for public use only. This part of the government vehicle reform encourages the public to supervise the public use of government vehicles reporting their private use to the relevant authorities, using readily available telephone numbers. In May 2015, Li Ming, the deputy director of the Development and Reform Commission (NDRC, *fazhan yu gage weiyuanhui*) of Guangdong Province, clarified that government vehicles left over after the reform would carry clear identifications, excluding those with unique purposes such as urban management vehicles. Although the vehicles' specific units were not displayed, citizens could easily identify and supervise government vehicles in any corner of the city.[25]

7.4.2 Social support

Public opinion on this innovation was the reformers' first and foremost concern. First, the public had not participated in the policymaking process for the innovation. The whole government vehicle reform policy process was kept secret from the public in Pingshan and other districts, as the government did not seek public participation at the scheme design stage. When asked, the policymakers confirmed that no person outside the bureaucratic system had participated in the policymaking process, meaning the government received no policy input from the public. Another interviewee expressed his concerns about this:

> *Personally, I surely hope the standard of subsidy could be a bit higher. On the other hand, I feel that there is something wrong about this policy because the whole process was carried out with no ordinary people's participation.*
>
> (LAI-2015-17)

Second, though the public was isolated from the government's policymaking, it did more or less know what was happening from insiders who expressed their views on the Internet and showed their support for the reform. The media reports on the reform of government vehicles usually started with the term "the long-awaited reform by the public."[26] Besides, the public also expressed their worries about the reform. The most prominent one was the concern that the civil servants would take the subsidies of the reform and, at the same time, continue to use the government vehicles.[27] Another point concerned the necessity to rationalize the regulation to restrict the use of government vehicles. For example, it was felt that the scheme had to do more to prevent alternative ways to abuse government vehicles. Accordingly, the public's requirements meant the reformers needed to make detailed regulations, particularly regarding abusive behaviors.[28]

Though the public did not have opportunities to participate directly, policymakers read newspapers and discussed public opinion when drafting the scheme, meaning public concerns indirectly helped improve it.

Besides public opinion, the views of civil servants who participated in or were affected by the reform also mattered. When a dozen government officials who contributed to or were affected by the reform were interviewed, they all agreed that most public officials backed the innovation. There were some fencesitters, particularly among those not affected by the reform, but there were no opponents:

> *Actually, most civil servants support this reform, because a large proportion of them did not have their own vehicles before this reform, which means they get a subsidy as a bonus. Those who own government vehicles are at least equal to or above the division-level head (chuji ganbu). In other words, the grassroots-level civil servants whose levels are equal to or below the section-level head (keji ganbu) did not enjoy the service of a government vehicle before the reform. The latter part of civil servants is the majority and naturally become the supporters of the government vehicle reform. They are most concerned about the standard of subsidy. The rest of the leading cadres will lose government vehicle service afterward; they are not really interested in the reform. They could no longer use government vehicles for free and have to pay extra money for their daily vehicle use, because the subsidy is not enough to cover their daily transportation fee.*
>
> (LAI-2015-16)

According to the Shenzhen reform scheme, officials at or above the deputy department level (*fu tingji*), such as the secretary of Pingshan District, were not required to participate in government vehicle reform and could keep their special vehicles as before.

> *For these leading cadres, they are non-stakeholders of this reform, thus have no motivation to fight for grassroots civil servants' interest. They are glad to launch the reform scheme as early as possible to get recognition from higher authorities. The other group of fencesitters is those who are not satisfied with the level of subsidy.*
>
> (LAI-2015-16)

From the interviews, the existence of three groups of civil servants could be identified based on their administrative levels. They held different views about the reform, as summarized in Table 7.2.

In a word, the higher an official's administrative level, the less they cared about the reform because they would not be affected by it. Most civil servants supported the innovation since it brought them a subsidy without loss. Thus, media reports described the reform as "a public consensus"[29] that won the

Table 7.2 Attitudes of civil servants toward the reform

Level of civil servants	*Vehicle status before the reform*	*Vehicle status after the reform*	*Personal view on the reform*	*Number of civil servants interviewed*
Equal to or above the deputy bureau level (*fu tingji ganbu*)	Enjoyed government-assigned vehicles (and in some cases owned private vehicles)	Kept their special vehicles or received subsidies	Neutral	1
Equal to or above the division-level head (*chuji ganbu*)	Enjoyed government-assigned vehicles (and some of them owned private vehicles)	Had no special vehicles and received subsidies	Negative	Less than 10
Equal to or below section-level head (*keji ganbu*)	Did not have government-assigned vehicles (and in most cases did not own private vehicles)	Received subsidies	Positive	Majority

Source: Compiled by the author from interviews conducted in Pingshan.

public's heart and got support from government officials. Social support laid the foundation for the reform's later smooth operation.

7.4.3 Organizational support

As in previous chapters, I define the organization as consisting of government institutions engaged in innovations and, in this case, government vehicle reform. China's bureaucratic system is characterized by a "*tiao-kuai* relationship" (條塊關係), meaning agencies must o seek a balance between horizontal and vertical power distribution (Mertha, 2005). Under this unique power distribution system, nothing can be decided or implemented without overcoming departmental disputes; thus, organizational support can determine the fate of the government vehicle reform. Unsurprisingly, the government vehicle reform leading group in Pingshan—a collaborative group comprised of civil servants from the Reform Office, the financial bureau, the human resource bureau, the development and reform bureau, the discipline and inspection commission, and other related departments—faced the same situation. Each bureau reported to its corresponding superior department while simultaneously working with other bureaus at the same level. Among all these bureaus, the Reform Office (改革辦公室) made the final decision. The leading group is a temporary organization with the power to organize the reform's ongoing situation while facing deep-rooted disputes among the participating departments.

During the interview, I asked whether these organizations worked well together in policymaking and implementation. A key member of the Reform

Office in charge of drafting the Pingshan scheme complained about the tension between "steering and rowing," a common phenomenon in policymaking and implementation:

> *We have good intentions, and we work well with other bureaus in the drafting period. When the policy falls to the ground, we have to face challenges. The problem is that we only have policymaking power, but not implementation power. After the policy is implemented, many things got done by other bureaus without notifying our office. We even have no idea about how many government vehicles have been kept in reality. We only have the number of government vehicles to be kept in theory according to our calculation. So, we have the leading role in name only and with no implementing power. It is really an offensive errand. Our office is not in charge of any government vehicle, has no financial power, and we are not clear with personnel establishment. Paradoxically, it is us that take the lead to make the reform scheme and have to answer to the higher authority.*
>
> (LAI-2015-18)

The interviewee expressed his concerns about how to negotiate with other bureaus. He found it difficult to promote the reform without higher-level authorities assigning power to the leading group. The reform also brought about extra work and inconvenience for other bureaus; for example, they had to hand in their government vehicles and calculate how many subsidies they should assign to existing civil servants. All these details then had to be confirmed and worked out under the leadership of the leading group.

Another interviewee, a staff member of the Reform Office, pointed out that in his eyes,

> *The key of this reform is to balance interests among various government departments. For example, when discussing the quota of vehicles each section could keep for necessary official use, the standard is vague according to the file. Then the dispute happens if one section could keep a vehicle for subsequent use, while the other one has none. The latter one would challenge the standard for necessary official duty. Another thing is that this innovation means extra work for other departments. They are not willing to cope with the leading group to finish this task as required.*
>
> (LAI-2015-16)

From the interview, we find that the organizations in charge of policymaking policy and implementation both did their jobs, working out a practical scheme together and finally implementing it. Practically, however, there existed some gaps between steering and rowing. For example, the departments involved in implementation focused only on their responsibilities and left some difficult tasks to the leading group. Many other sections bargained to advance their interests. As a result, the leading group had to organize meetings with the departments involved to deal with such unfinished tasks as the reallocation of drivers.

Despite these conflicts, the involved departments had to work together to achieve the same goal. They organized regular meetings to discuss the difficulties and offer solutions, as did the municipal-level leading group. According to the interviewee from the Reform Office, his department led the negotiation and pushed the innovation forward, balancing the departments' interests by repeatedly revising the scheme.

7.5 Conclusion

The reform eventually achieved success. Its first achievement was a 10% reduction in expenditures on government vehicles in Pingshan, well above the average in other provinces (7.88%). Thus, the reformers had met the reform's primary objective—saving public money. The second achievement was the reform's smooth process, as no significant conflict was detected during its planning and implementation. The third achievement concerned the reform's sustainability. Since the reform, civil servants have adopted new means of transportation instead of relying government vehicles and are receiving regular subsidies. With these conditions having been met, we can conclude that the innovation is successful.

Compared with the other two cases (Jiangmen and Hengqin), the reform of government vehicles met the greatest number of institutional conditions, thus ultimately achieving success. First, the reform received support from superior government agencies. On several occasions at the beginning of the reform, the leaders of Guangdong Province expressed support for the innovation at the municipal level.[30] Later, during the reform process, the central government's early move pushed the innovation steadily forward. Moreover, the reform had the public's understanding and agreement, as people had been calling for this innovation for years. At the same time, civil servants could accept this change as long as they got to benefit from the reform. These supports created a suitable external environment for the reform, while the key internal factor, organizational support, ensured its steady implementation. Together, these factors led the reform to final success.

However, the leading group's work continues. Group members are following up by preparing to buy the customized public transportation service and convert it into a free shuttle between the downtown area and Pingshan to reduce civil servants' commuting time.[31] Another tough job is managing retired government vehicles. Thus far, the leading group has organized three rounds of public auctions in which most of the retired vehicles were sold to citizens. The remaining vehicles are now locked in a rented warehouse for emergency use. Those wanting to use these vehicles must apply to the local DIC for approval. As for the drivers, those younger than 60 were transferred to other government positions, such as security guards; those older than 60 retired five years ahead of time.

The reform has follow-up problems, though it is a success. One year after the reform, I returned to Pingshan and observed the "post-reform" situation. The reformers reflected on the innovation, noting that civil servants were most concerned with the subsidy imbalance, which they described as the phenomenon of "three hundreds." Compared to their peers working in city centers, civil servants working in the suburbs must commute another 100 kilometers per day, pay another 100 yuan for highway fees and gas costs, and add 100 additional minutes to their daily commutes. As such, they desired higher subsidies than those given to downtown civil servants.

Notes

1 The three public expenditures account for 10% of the 2012 annual fiscal revenue in China. See http://finance.ifeng.com/news/macro/20130325/7817063.shtml. Accessed in August 2015.
2 See http://www.chinanews.com/gn/2013/01-04/4454507.shtml Accessed in August 2015.
3 The RCCK proposed to reform the expenditure on government vehicles in China. See http://auto.163.com/special/gongchegaige/ Accessed in August 2015.
4 See http://gb.corp.163.com/gb/about/overview.html Accessed in August 2015.
5 See http://news.163.com/special/gcggfa/ Accessed in August 2015.
6 Government vehicles consume nearly 300 billion yuan. See http://finance.sina.com.cn/china/20150304/232521645929.shtml. Accessed in August 2015.
7 See http://finance.sina.com.cn/china/20150304/232521645929.shtml.
8 Source: http://news.163.com/special/gcggfa/. Accessed in August, 2015.
9 They are Jiangsu, Hubei, Anhui, Tianjin, Inner Mongolia, Ningxia, Qinghai, Shanxi, Hebei, Chongqing, Hunan, Yunnan, Shandong, and Henan.
10 The central leading group is affiliated to the National Development and Reform Commission, which includes officials from other departments such as the CDIC, the State Department, and other related central departments.
11 Twenty provinces have submitted their schemes of government vehicle reform. See https://kknews.cc/zh-hk/news/x5z6gmg.html. Accessed in October 2015.
12 Twenty provinces submitted the schemes of government vehicle reform to the central government. See http://bingodu.com/news/143797.html. Accessed in September 2015.
13 Government vehicle reform: reducing 62% vehicles and saving 7.88% public expenditure. See http://m.21jingji.com/article/20150916/herald/509a34b0244c821ffd3b4001147fbdb3.html. Accessed in September 2015.
14 See http://www.chinanews.com/gn/2012/08-08/4090707.shtml. Accessed in August 2015.
15 See http://www.360doc.com/content/14/0424/18/155881_371780821.shtml. Accessed in September 2015.
16 Opinions from official of Guangdong Province on Shenzhen government vehicle reform. See http://www.china.com.cn/chinese/zhuanti/gchgg/731670.htm. Accessed in September 2015.
17 http://news.ifeng.com/gundong/detail_2014_03/12/34672771_0.shtml. Accessed in August 2015.
18 Shenzhen enacted government vehicle reform yesterday. See http://www.yicai.com/news/3610272.html. Accessed in August 2015.
19 Reform is Shenzhen's lifeline. See http://www.psxq.gov.cn/main/a/2015/c16/a30325_50254.shtml Accessed in September 2015.
20 See http://www.nfmedia.com/jtdt/jtxw/201502/t20150211_366325.html. Accessed in September 2015.
21 Scheme of Shenzhen Government vehicle reform 2015. See http://www.xuexila.com/zhichang/zhengce/166324.html. Accessed in August 2015.
22 The Comprehensive Guide to Push Forward the Reform of Government Vehicle Management. See http://fanfu.people.com.cn/n/2014/0717/c64371-25291927.html. Accessed in September 2015.

23 Guangxi DRC http://xbkfs.ndrc.gov.cn/mzfz/201608/t20160809_814246.html.

24 Shenzhen has 10 districts: Futian, Luohu, Nanshan, Yantian, Bao'an, Longgang, Longhua, Guangming, Pingshan, and Dapeng. Among them, the former six districts were located in central areas, and the latter four districts are on the relative outskirts.

25 See http://finance.ifeng.com/a/20160728/14649250_0.shtml. Accessed in September 2015.

26 See http://news.sina.com.cn/c/2014-03-12/052029685527.shtml. Accessed in September 2015.

27 Shenzhen government vehicle reform was criticized on its subsidies. See http://finance.people.com.cn/n/2015/0403/c1004-26793433.html. Accessed in September 2015.

28 Government vehicle reform in Shenzhen. http://www.qstheory.cn/zhuanqu/bkjx/2015-04/05/c_1114875981.htm. Accessed in September 2015.

29 See http://www.chinacity.org.cn/cshb/cssy/287979.html. Also, see http://www.qstheory.cn/special/5684/yzxylgcgg/6071/201109/t20110905_108177.html. Both accessed in September 2015.

30 Discussions on Guangdong government vehicle reform. See http://www.360doc.com/content/09/0824/21/155881_5225485.shtml. Accessed in September 2015.

31 One year after Shenzhen government vehicle reform: an observation. See http://epaper.oeeee.com/epaper/H/html/2015-05/13/content_3419267.htm?div=-1. Accessed in August 2015.

8 Conclusion

This study's primary purpose has been to see how the war against corruption in China has taken place and assess its current bottom-up efforts. Second, it has explored how and why some local anti-corruption innovations succeeded under China's current political framework, while others failed. The findings indicate that the survival and development of local anti-corruption innovations are institutionally constrained, depending on whether they received political, organizational, and social support.

8.1 Summary of Findings

This study has three main findings.

First, while anti-corruption innovations have become increasingly common at local levels in recent years, insufficient scholarly attention has been paid to this issue. During its economic transformation period, China employed top-down anti-corruption measures, with the central government playing a leading role in organizing nationwide anti-corruption rectification.

However, a growing number of anti-corruption innovations have taken place at local levels, signaling that local governments have actively moved to control corruption. This trend also suggests that central-level policy may not meet local needs. Regional differences cannot be ignored, and no one-size-fits-all central policy exists. Since the 2000s, numerous local anti-corruption innovations, some of which have even expanded to other localities, have contributed to local experience. For example, the first government to experiment with property declarations for government officials was Aletai City, Xinjiang; later, Cixi, Zhejiang Province, and Liuyang, Hunan Province, took similar measures. The asset declaration system has not yet been adopted nationwide due to political sensitivity, but these localities were allowed to choose between innovating, implementing central policies, or adopting technical tools for integrity building. Those who intend to make institutional changes usually face difficulties and are constrained by existing political conditions.

Beyond the 437 cases collected and presented in this study, many more recent anti-corruption innovations have been analyzed by other scholars

DOI: 10.4324/9781003112105-8

(He, 2000; Li, 2015; Wang, 2009; Zhuang, 2011). Li (2015) summarized three types of local anti-corruption innovations based on central government approaches: innovations initiated by local governments, accepted by the central government, and diffused to other localities; central policies piloted at local levels for later adoption by other local governments; and innovations attempted by local governments without central government comment.

This leads to the second finding: local anti-corruption innovations are difficult to make and sustain. They require both external and internal support, as summarized in the following formula based on my case analyses in Chapters 5, 6, and 7:

Successful anti-corruption innovation
= political approval + organizational endorsement + social support

To succeed, a new policy initiative in the anti-corruption domain must have solid and sustainable political, organizational, and social foundations. Though local governments may have more autonomy in making initiatives, whether they can successfully carry them out depends on factors beyond their control.

By political approval, I mean political and legal support from higher authorities. In the case of anti-corruption innovations, this usually involves approval from upper-level DICs. For example, all four cases in this study were supervised by Guangdong DIC, whose endorsement had to be obtained before the innovations could be attempted. The level from which an endorsement should come depends on the situation. For example, the Hengqin case required the central government's blessing for its smooth implementation, while the provincial government largely determined the Jiangmen case.

By organizational endorsement, I refer to horizontal support from the departments involved in an innovation. For example, the Shenzhen leading group needed support from the Reform Office, the Bureau of Finance, and the Development and Reform Commission at the same level to design and implement its policies on government vehicle reform. Social support means getting positive social reflections from the public. The Jiangmen case is a living example of how innovations that receive harsh public criticism can fail.

This study provides a detailed analysis of the four cases under different institutional conditions. All were initiated in recent years and represent local efforts at anti-corruption innovation. Table 8.1 lists four anti-corruption innovations discussed in the case study and provides key information about each case's three kinds of support and outcomes.

From the table, it is clear that the Jiangmen and Hengqin cases both encountered institutional voids in their innovative processes, while the Qianhai and Shenzhen cases did not. The Qianhai and Shenzhen cases had sufficient institutional support and were successful, while the Jiangmen case had the least support and failed soon after it was enacted. The Hengqin case, however, continues to struggle to sustain political and social support while lacking

Table 8.1 Analytical frameworks of four cases

Local anti-corruption Innovation Case	*Political approval*	*Organizational endorsement*	*Social support*	*Outcome*
Integrity Pension Fund in Jiangmen		✓		Failure
Integrated Office of Integrity in Zhuhai Hengqin	✓		✓	Ongoing with difficulties
Qianhai Anticorruption Bureau	✓	✓	✓	Success
Reform of government vehicle management in Shenzhen	✓	✓	✓	Success

Source: Compiled by the author.

organizational support. In what follows, I briefly introduce each case and indicate the interrelationship between various institutional constraints and the innovations' different fates.

The four cases had entirely different fates, though they were all carried out in Guangdong Province and started in the same period. The Jiangmen case aimed at setting up an Integrity Pension Fund to ensure honest government in 2011. The idea was initially supported by the DIC of Guangdong Province but was terminated by higher authorities in the face of firm public opposition. In the Hengqin case, the provincial government endorsed Hengqin DIC's plan to build an integrated office of integrity in 2013, despite strong suspicions it was unconstitutional, forcing it to deal with conflicting organizational interests while carrying out the innovation. The Qianhai case made a similar attempt to reorganize the anti-corruption agency but avoided the problem the Hengqin Integrity Office encountered by placing the integrity office under direct municipal government supervision, thereby minimizing departmental conflict. So far, it has functioned well. The Shenzhen case of reforming government vehicle management, which began in 2014 and faced no significant opposition, is both the most recent and successful of the four innovations.

Interpreting the four cases leads to a third point, i.e., that the three elements of institutional support do not necessarily carry equal weight. Senior political levels have veto power over local anti-corruption innovations, meaning political support is the most crucial factor. Local policymakers made it clear that without affirmation from higher authorities, innovations at local levels would not even be put on the policy agenda, let alone see smooth implementation. The Jiangmen Case failed due to a lack of continued support from the higher authority (in this case, the DIC of Guangdong Province), although public opposition might be the underlying reason for its termination.

Social and organizational support rank behind political support but are also essential to anti-corruption innovations. The conflict of interest among various institutions was a great challenge to the Hengqin case. In the beginning, there was a high expectation for the Integrated Integrity Office by Guangdong DIC, since it seemed to be a thorough institutional reform aiming to build an independent anti-corruption agency with general functions. However, it withered away due to its later failure to balance organizational interests, and its impact became significantly weakened.

It should also be noted that anti-corruption innovations are not the same as other local innovations mentioned in the Introduction. Most anti-corruption innovations affect vested interests and thus encounter more barriers than other innovations. For example, the Property Declaration System touches upon the interests of the hierarchical system. If the system is built and implemented, those covered by the policy will have to reveal their properties to the public. Entrenched resistance to change is why one interviewee described the fight against corruption as "a battle between life and death" (生死攸關).

This is not to say that other innovations, such as economic and social management innovations, are easy to make, just that anti-corruption innovations are those that local governments are least likely to make. Those who volunteer to make anti-corruption innovations face challenges from three institutional voids: political approval, organizational endorsement, and social support.

All in all, local anti-corruption innovations, especially those sensitive ones, are highly constrained by both external factors largely beyond their control (e.g., political and social conditions surrounding the institutions making innovations) and internal factors like the degree of organizational cooperation among the institutions initiating the innovations.

8.2 Theoretical Implications

Scholarly attention has turned to anti-corruption work in China in recent decades. China's anti-corruption practice is now experiencing an "institutional turn" (Gong, 2011: 671) from campaign-style anti-corruption enforcement to institutionalized integrity management. Wedeman pointed out that campaign-style enforcement may have contributed to the "intensification" of corruption (Wedeman, 2005). Quade established a causal link between anti-corruption campaigns and economic austerity rounds and questioned the real intention behind China's anti-corruption efforts (Quade, 2007). The existing literature mainly focuses on national-level anti-corruption programs, rather than local-level anti-corruption measures aimed at enhancing local integrity management. As such, local governments' role in anti-corruption reform is understudied, with only a few scholars (Wang, 2009; Gong, 2011; Gong, 2014; Zhu, 2008) touching upon their motivations and effectiveness. My study fills this gap in the literature by examining local efforts at controlling corruption, especially innovative measures.

As mentioned in the Introduction, innovations run institutional risks, particularly anti-corruption innovations. This research combines two important topics—innovation and anti-corruption—and looks into their institutional restrictions. Combining these two topics enriches our understanding of one particular type of local innovation, i.e., anti-corruption innovation. Not much attention has been paid to these innovations for various reasons, such as the difficulty of accessing interviewees and the lack of data. From this perspective, this study also adds empirical evidence to the study of local integrity management systems, their barriers, and corresponding solutions.

From the theoretical perspective, this is also a new effort to apply an institutional void perspective to anti-corruption studies. As stated in Chapter 4 (theoretical framework), the institutional void perspective has been used to analyze strategies adopted for national development(Ngo, 2009), social movements (Ngo, 2015), local management (Yep, 2015), and democratic transitions (Bedock, 2013). This study, however, analyzes anti-corruption innovations from an institutional void perspective involving three dimensions: political, organizational, and social. The reason for adopting the institutional void perspective in this research is that the authors mentioned above tend to relate policies' success or strategic failure to their political space. By analyzing three institutional voids, my study makes clear the importance of "institutional foundations" for understanding the survival and sustainability of anti-corruption innovations.

This study has theoretical implications for corruption studies. The three factors identified herein as contributing to the fate of anti-corruption innovations—political approval, organizational endorsement, and social support—correspond to some major debates in the existing literature on corruption, such as the role of political will in controlling corruption, the effectiveness of anti-corruption agencies, and public engagement in anti-corruption activities.

8.2.1 Political will and corruption control

The first topic is the impact of political will on corruption control. Post et al. (2010) defined political will based on a review of previous definitions, determining that an operational concept of political will must have four components: a sufficient set of decision-makers; a common understanding of a particular problem on the formal agenda; commitment to supporting; and a commonly perceived and potentially effective policy solution.

Scholars also attempt to determine to what extent political will influences the outcome of anti-corruption efforts. Brinkerhoff (2000) analyzed political will and its relationship with the design, initiation, and pursuit of anti-corruption activities. He referred to political will as "the commitment of actors to undertake actions to achieve a set of objectives—in this case, anti-corruption policies and programs—and to sustain the costs of those actions over time" (Brinkerhoff, 2000). Based on this list of characteristics, he argued that political will directly impacts support for anti-corruption reform and the design and implementation of reform policies. Quah (1999) viewed political will as the key to the success of anti-corruption activities. He classified East Asian countries based on the extent of their political will and anti-corruption measures to determine their anti-corruption effectiveness (Quah, 2006).

Then it comes down to how to obtain political will. Fritzen (2006) pointed out the "orthodox paradox" for political will in anti-corruption activities, as shown in the case of Vietnam. Unlike the authors mentioned above, he noted that political will might be affected by authoritarian institutions and, in consequence, negatively affect the feasibility and sustainability of anti-corruption efforts.

My study contributes to the scholarly discussion of political will by showing that innovation is hardly possible without political approval and support. This parallels the empirical findings in this study, i.e., that anti-corruption reforms are not possible without political approval and support. Political will is the engine of anti-corruption reform. The case of Jiangmen has made it clear that it is not easy to obtain and, once obtained, may yet be lost. Higher-level authorities tend to take a wait-and-see attitude towards bottom-up initiatives or innovations before fully supporting and allocating resources to an innovation. The sustainability of political will is affected by the innovation's efficiency and public feedback.

8.2.2 Effectiveness of anti-corruption agencies

The second critical issue in anti-corruption practice is the effectiveness of anti-corruption agencies. An anti-corruption agency is viewed as an "integrity warrior" in corruption control, which plays a key role in improving integrity building. Scholars summarize the characteristics of some successful models, such as the ICAC and the CPIB in Hong Kong and Singapore (Choi, 2009; Meagher, 2005), and agree that the autonomy of anti-corruption agencies is contributes prominently to their effectiveness (Johnston, 1999).

There is a dispute about whether to set single or multiple agencies at the national level to achieve the goal of corruption control. The answer may vary with the particular condition of a country. Some Nordic countries, including Finland, Norway, and Sweden, which have been ranked at the top of Transparency International's (TI) Corruption Perception Index (CPI) list for years, do not even have a dedicated anti-corruption agency. However, among those countries that have anti-corruption agencies, it is believed that a single anti-corruption agency functions better than multiple agencies. Furthermore, the more independent the agency is, the more likely it is to succeed in fighting corruption. Besides independence, the agencies must command public respect and be credible, transparent, and fearless. They must be subject to review by a free press and civil society and be accountable to the public (Pope & Vogl, 2000).

In China, as discussed in this study, the recent attempt to reform anti-corruption agencies by merging them into one follows this line of thinking, as it facilitates information exchange, streamlines decision-making processes, and prevents unnecessary interagency disputes.

8.2.3 *Civil society engagement in anti-corruption activities*

The third theoretical implication is civil society engagement in anti-corruption activities. There has long been a discussion on the role of the public in anti-corruption work or, to put it in a larger picture, the pros and cons of top-down and bottom-up approaches in fighting corruption. However, one thing has been evident in governance studies: public involvement contributes to corruption control (Themudo, 2013). Kaufmann (1998) referred to civil society participation as "the unfinished agenda" for the next stage of anti-corruption efforts. He agreed with the current research on this topic that the involvement of civil society in anti-corruption practice increases the possibility of keeping a country clean but stressed the need to go one step further to make civil participation operate more efficiently. He provided some suggestions on strengthening the role of civil society, such as equipping civil society with technologies, seeking allies in the bureaucratic system, empowering women, and so on.

Although these suggestions might work, the reality in developing countries is that civil society's evolution is minimal. Civil society's engagement in anti-corruption policymaking and innovations is low in China. The public is often kept outside governments' agenda setting and policy processes. As is obvious in the Jiangmen and Shenzhen cases, the public was not allowed to participate in the policy process and could only express their opinions after the fact via the Internet. The public alone has limited impact on corruption control and good governance. As pointed out by Ackerman (2013), civil society's involvement in anti-corruption usually takes the form of collective action, instead of participating in peaceful policymaking, due to lack of permission by the government.

Under China's current situation, the key to unlocking the capacity of the public is to empower local governments. As the middle level of government, local governments are channels between the national government and the public. They can effectively raise civil awareness of and engagement in anti-corruption practices, own critical local resources, have better access to local information, and are most likely to find solutions to local corruption.

As Gong (2015) suggested, we may need to take a further step forward from the local levels' initiation toward the socially based innovations. In that way, innovations may sustain themselves. The root of the success of anti-corruption innovation may lie in social efforts instead of relying on the government to play a solo role. There are some options for the future development of anti-corruption measures, including bringing the central government back in, linking the central and local together, or stimulating local enthusiasm. Local governments could do much more to make the public's voice heard.

8.3 Anti-corruption Practices at a Crossroads

This research also has practical implications in terms of policy recommendations. The future of anti-corruption innovations at local levels is a mixed picture. The dynamics for local governments to make innovative anti-corruption policies are not as strong as before, especially after the 18th National Congress of the CPC, when the central government re-centralized its anti-corruption policymaking. The anti-corruption storms of "shooting tigers and beating flies (打老虎, 拍蒼蠅)" signaled a top-down approach to controlling corruption. It seems that local anti-corruption innovations are experiencing a low ebb since Xi came to power. In this context, analyzing the dynamics and mechanisms of anti-corruption innovations at local levels has policy implications for future corruption control strategies. This study has provided a report of how local governments have made their efforts in integrity management in various ways. Not limited to presenting the overall situation of current local anticorruption innovations, the study has also pointed out the dilemmas facing and institutional constraints on local anti-corruption innovations. All these findings have policy implications. For example, the central government should allocate more resources to support local anti-corruption innovations. The CDIC may also improve its understanding of how local governments are institutionally constrained when making innovations; hence, more support should be provided.

Besides the overall political environment, the nature of innovation, especially anti-corruption innovations, contributes to local governments' hesitation to make initiatives. First, unlike other reforms, anti-corruption innovations are low priorities for local governments to achieve among a set of targets they have to pursue. Those goals include economic performance, social stability, urban development, etc. The importance of anti-corruption innovations also ranks behind social stability goals. Although successful innovations serve as bonuses when they do a good job and get recognized by the higher authorities, innovations naturally carry risks.

Despite low enthusiasm at local levels for anti-corruption innovation, the battle against corruption is still going on in China. The central government has taken some dramatic moves towards controlling and preventing corruption. One is the central decision to establish a National Supervision Commission (hereafter, NSC), with local experimentation being carried out first. The other is the theoretical proposal of a "particular integrity zone," advanced by scholars in integrity studies.

In November 2016, the central government announced its plan to reform China's entire integrity management system by setting up an overarching institution—the National Supervision Commission (NSC)—to build unified anti-corruption work under the CPC's leadership. The reform is being conducted at the institutional level by integrating several anti-corruption agencies into new commissions, such as the Beijing Supervision Committee (BSC), which merged three separate institutions—the Discipline Inspection Commission, the Bureau of Supervision, and the Anti-corruption Bureau—into procuratorates to expand the scope of inspection, enhance supervision, and fully cover officials exercising public power. The new commission is expected to establish a centralized, unified, authoritative, and efficient supervisory system, fulfill anti-corruption duties, and deepen the Party's integrity building. The reform also aims to strengthen the authority of anti-corruption agencies in China and ensure anti-corruption agencies have the power to search, arrest, and prosecute.

To effectively implement the plan, the central government decided to run pilot programs in three localities (Beijing, Jiangxi, and Zhejiang Province) by setting up local Supervision Commissions in 2017. Combining the discipline inspection commission, supervision branch, and inspection organ was a historic breakthrough.

The reform and its application may solve some current dilemmas facing anti-corruption agencies, such as the lack of a central 'hub' institution to facilitate cooperation among anti-corruption institutions. The functions of the various institutions with anti-corruption responsibility overlap and sometimes even conflict, thereby wasting anti-corruption resources. Judicial and administrative procedures for handling corruption cases could be streamlined by combining departments to increase the efficiency of their anti-corruption work and reallocate anti-corruption resources to avoid duplication of efforts. It would also simplify integrity-building procedures, since DICs and supervision organs operate in parallel when dealing with suspected fraud cases. The difference between the two agencies is that the DICs mainly deal with the misconduct of the CPC members while supervision organs handle cases concerning state officials.

Gong (2008) pointed out that DICs are internal CPC institutions conducting investigations and applying appropriate disciplinary measures where Party discipline has been violated (Gong, 2008: 140). Supervision organs are state organs and usually work in parallel with the DICs at the same level. The DICs and supervision organs work jointly on corruption control and prevention.

The organized structure and personnel are in place but have not yet been open to the public.[1] The new trend confirms the central government's support for conducting structural reform to the anti-corruption agencies. The central leaders decided to try out new commissions at local levels first, indicating they value local experiences. The logic of this reform is similar to the local anti-corruption innovations discussed in this study, especially in the Hengqin Case. They are both directed at the restructuring of anti-corruption agencies. However, the Hengqin case was initiated and implemented entirely by the local government. On the other hand, the NSC reform shows the effort to combine top-down and bottom-up anti-corruption practices, which may represent the future trend of anti-corruption reform in China. This new development further proves that without support from higher authorities, such as the central government's endorsement, local innovations could hardly make substantial progress.

8.4 Limitations of this Study and Future Research Agenda

In this study, I adopted a qualitative case study method. Information was gathered from interviews, media reports, and official documents. The first limitation is the geographical scope of selected cases. For accessibility reasons, case selection was confined to Guangdong Province, although nationwide information on anti-corruption innovations is provided as background in Chapter 2. Four different cases at the municipal level in Guangdong are analyzed in great detail in Chapters 5, 6, and 7. Nonetheless, according to Hodkinson (2001), findings from case studies are not generalizable in the conventional sense. By definition, case studies can make no claims to be typical. Furthermore, because the sample is small and idiosyncratic, there is no way to establish the probability that the data are representative of a larger population.

All conclusions of this research are based on two to three years of observation, and case studies aim to discover new variables, new patterns, and new trends. Hence, my attempts are exploratory. This study explores cases to answer a "how" question, i.e., how to achieve successful anti-corruption innovations under given political conditions. I tried to capture the main features of these cases and analyze them with the proposed theoretical framework. It is also true that policy innovation tends to be a temporary phenomenon and is subject to change. Policy innovations appear or disappear with the changing political environment. Therefore, the findings from this study are not necessarily valid in other settings.

The limitation of this study is nevertheless leaves room for further research. For example, quantitative methods may be adopted to examine a larger number of local innovation cases and help find the independent variables contributing to anti-corruption innovations' outcomes. Such variables may include the demographic characteristics of local ACA leaders, local conditions like economic growth levels, and the intensity of local corruption conditions. Another possible approach is to make comparative studies of local anti-corruption innovations. Specifically, one could expand the time and geographical location to select a larger range of cases for further studies, which may help find historical and regional differences in innovations. Both approaches are on my future research agenda.

Another limitation is that this study did not check the quality of the innovations, which is an important consideration concerning their results. There is no denying that sometimes internal factors weigh more than external support. For example, the Hengqin case ran far more risks than other innovations because it broke the current policy framework by attempting to reorganize an anti-corruption agency. The policy design in the Hengqin case had to consider the existing institutional setting to achieve the ACA's smooth structural change. Although this study does not focus on the quality of innovations, that does not mean quality is not significant.

One more limitation lies in the analytical framework. The framework contains three institutional conditions for an innovation: political approval, organizational endorsement, and social support. Among them, political approval is the most essential. However, interactions among the three pillars to constrain the development of local innovations should be explored. Future studies will benefit from an in-depth analysis of internal factors in successful or failed innovations.

Finally, it has been suggested that many local governments in China were interested in learning from the experiences of Hong Kong and Singapore in controlling corruption, but encountered difficulties due to China's political setting. For example, the Integrity Pension Funds implemented in Liuyang County in 2003, Xiacheng District of Hangzhou City and Cixi City in 2005, and Jiangmen in 2010 all borrowed ideas from the Hong Kong experience, as stated in Chapter 5. Why did the Fund fail in these mainland China localities but succeed in Hong Kong and Singapore, which also have majority-Chinese populations? Future studies could compare the Fund's implementation in various locations in mainland China and Hong Kong.

Note

1 What have Beijing, Zhejiang, and Shanxi Supervision Commission done in the past three months? Source: http://news.sinovision.net/politics/201702/00400384.htm. Accessed in 19 February 2017.

Appendix 1
Interview Coding Book

The coding format (e.g., LAI-2014-12) used in this study implies three layers of information. "LAI" represents the research subject "local anti-corruption innovations," followed by the year when the interview was conducted ("2014"). The final number "12" indicates that it is the 12th interview. For more detailed information about the interviews, see the attached list of the interview.

Interview no.	*Interview code*	*Interviewee*
Interview 1	LAI-2011-1	An official from Jiangmen DIC
Interview 2	LAI-2011-2	An official from Jiangmen DIC
Interview 3	LAI-2011-3	An official from the Municipal Bureau of Finance, Jiangmen
Interview 4	LAI-2011-4	The Vice Party Secretary of Jiangmen DIC
Interview 5	LAI-2011-5	An official from the Municipal Bureau of Labor and Social Security Bureau, Jiangmen
Interview 6	LAI-2011-6	An official from the Municipal Fiscal Bureau of Jiangmen
Interview 7	LAI-2011-7	An official from the department of propaganda of Jiangmen
Interview 8	LAI-2011-8	An official from Jiangmen DIC
Interview 9	LAI-2011-9	A Municipal Party Committee Member of Jiangmen City
Interview 10	LAI-2015-10	An official from the Qianhai Anti-corruption Bureau (QAB)
Interview 11	LAI-2014-11	The Vice Director of the Hengqin Integrity Office (IMO)
Interview 12	LAI-2014-12	The Director of IMO
Interview 13	LAI-2014-13	A standing member of the Party Committee from the DIC of Zhuhai
Interview 14	LAI-2014-14	An official from the Bureau of corruption prevention, the DIC of Zhuhai
Interview 15	LAI-2015-15	A clerk of Pingshan Reform Office
Interview 16	LAI-2015-16	A clerk of Pingshan Wisdom Community Office
Interview 17	LAI-2015-17	A clerk of Pingshan Reform Office

(*Continued*)

Interview no.	*Interview code*	*Interviewee*
Interview 18	LAI-2015-18	A clerk of Pingshan Investigation Office
Interview 19	LAI-2014-19	A scholar from Fudan University, Shanghai
Interview 20	LAI-2014-20	A scholar from Sun Yat-sun University, Guangzhou
Interview 21	LAI-2015-21	A scholar from Tsinghua University, Beijing
Interview 22	LAI-2015-22	An official from the DIC of Beijing Construction Engineering Group
Interview 23	LAI-2015-23	An official from the Party Committee of Beijing Construction Engineering Group
Interview 24	LAI-2014-24	An official from Shanghai DIC

Appendix 2
List of Rules and Regulations on Government Integrity (in Chinese)

序號	法律規定	頒布年份
1	《關於嚴禁黨政機關和黨政幹部經商、辦企業的決定》	1984
2	《中國共產黨紀律處分條例(試行)》	1997
3	《公務人員管理命令》(香港)	1997
4	《中華人民共和國公務員法》	2006
5	《八項規定》	2012
6	《廣東省預防腐敗條例》	2014
7	《中國共產黨廉潔自律準則》	2015

Bibliography

Ackerman J. M. (2013). Rethinking the international anti-corruption agenda: Civil society, human rights and democracy. *American University International Law Review*. 29: 293.

Anechiarico F. (2009). Protecting integrity at the local level: The role of anti-corruption and public management networks. *Crime, Law and Social Change*. 53(1): 79–95. http://doi.org/10.1007/s10611-009-9216-y

Florini, A. M., Lai, H., & Tan, Y. (2012). *China experiments: From local innovations to national reform*. Washington, D.C.: Brookings Institution Press.

Bardhan P., & Mookherjee D. (2006). *Decentralization and local governance in developing countries: A comparative perspective* (Vol. 1). The MIT Press.

Baldridge J. V., & Burnham R. A. (1975). Organizational innovation: Individual, organizational, and environmental impacts. *Administrative Science Quarterly*. 20(2): 165–176.

Bedock C. (2013). Fill in the void? The politics of institutional reform in times of democratic crisis in Ireland. In Müller-Rommel F. and Casal Bértoa F. (eds). *Party politics and democracy in Europe: Essays in honour of Peter Mair*. Abingdon; New York: Routledge, pp. 34–49. http://hdl.handle.net/1814/37090

Bengtsson P. (1999). Multiple Case Studies, Spring, 1–9. Retrieved from http://citeseerx.ist.psu.edu/viewdoc/summary?doi=10.1.1.30.9769

Brinkerhoff D. W. (2000). Assessing political will for anti-corruption efforts: An analytic framework. *Public Administration and Development*. 20(3): 239–252.

Bengtsson P. (1999). Multiple Case Studies – Not just more data points ?! Spring, 1–9. Retrieved from http://citeseerx.ist.psu.edu/viewdoc/summary?doi=10.1.1.30.9769

Birney M. (2014). Decentralization and veiled corruption under China's "rule of mandates." *World Development*. 53: 55–67. http://doi.org/10.1016/j.worlddev.2013.01.006

Boehmke F. J., & Witmer R. (2004). Disentangling diffusion: The effects of social learning and economic competition on state policy innovation and expansion. *Political Research Quarterly*. 57(1): 39–51.

Borins S. (2002). Leadership and innovation in the public sector. *Leadership & Organization Development Journal*. 23(8): 467–476. http://doi.org/10.1108/01437730210449357

Chen S. (2003). Supervision culture, mechanism and official corruption crime. *Journal of Political Science and Law*. 20: 11–13.

Chen T. (2003). The characteristics of institutional innovation of local government in China. *Journal of Guangdong Institute of Public Administration*. 15: 15–18.

Cheng J. (2000). Guangdong's challenges: Organizational streamlining, economic restructuring and anti-corruption. *Pacific Affairs*. 73(1): 9–35. http://www.jstor.org/stable/2672282

Chien S.-S. (2007). Institutional innovations, asymmetric decentralization, and local economic development: A case study of Kunshan, in post-Mao China. *Environment and Planning C: Government and Policy*. 25(2): 269–290. http://doi.org/10.1068/c0558

Choi J.-W. (2009). Institutional structures and effectiveness of anti-corruption agencies: A comparative analysis of South Korea and Hong Kong. *Asian Journal of Political Science*. 17(2): 195–214. http://doi.org/10.1080/02185370903077485

Chunying W. (2009). Anti-corruption innovations at the local level in China since the reform and opening up policy. *New Horizons*. 208–214.

Cohen W. M., & Levinthal D. A. (1990). Absorptive capacity: A new perspective on learning and innovation. *Administrative Science Quarterly*, 128–152.

Cooke P., & Uranga M. G. (1997). Regional innovation systems: Institutional and organisational dimensions. *Research Policy*. 26(4–5): 475–491. https://doi.org/10.1016/S0048-7333(97)00025-5

De Sousa L. (2010). Anti-corruption agencies: Between empowerment and irrelevance. *Crime, Law and Social Change*. 53(1): 5–22. http://doi.org/10.1007/s10611-009-9211-3

Deng X., Zhang L., & Leverentz A. (2010). Official corruption during China's economic transition: Historical patterns, characteristics, and government reactions. *Journal of Contemporary Criminal Justice*. 26(1), 72–88. http://doi.org/10.1177/1043986209350302

Dickson B. J. (2000). Cooptation and corporatism in China: The logic of party adaptation. *Political Science Quarterly*. 115(4): 517–540. http://www.jstor.org/stable/2657608

Dong B., & Torgler B. (2013). Causes of corruption: Evidence from China. *China Economic Review*. 26(1): 152–169. http://doi.org/10.1016/j.chieco.2012.09.005

Edquist C. (Ed.). (1997). *Systems of innovation: Technologies, institutions, and organizations*. London: Psychology Press.

Eisenberger R., Armeli S., Rexwinkel B., Lynch P. D., & Rhoades L. (2001). Reciprocation of perceived organizational support. *Journal of Applied Psychology*. 86(1): 42.

Eisenhard K. (1989). Building theories from case study research. *Academy of Management Review*. 14: 532–550.

El W. J. (2011). Typology and characteristics of government innovations: A multi-case study of winning programs of the innovations and excellence in Chinese local governance. *Journal of Public Management*. 8: 94–103.

Fagerberg J., Mowery D. C., & Nelson R. R. (Eds.). (2005). *The Oxford handbook of innovation*. Oxford University Press.

Fagerberg J. (2006). Innovation: A guide to the literature. In Fagerberg, J., & Mowery, D. C. (eds). *The Oxford handbook of innovation*. Oxford University Press, pp. 1–22.

Fan C. S., Lin C., & Treisman D. (2009). Political decentralization and corruption: Evidence from around the world. *Journal of Public Economics*. 93(1–2): 14–34. http://doi.org/10.1016/j.jpubeco.2008.09.001

Feizhou Z. (2009). Championship system in China. *Sociology Research*, 1–23.

Feng Y. (2011). Current Chinese folk anti-corruption website and reflecting on its orderly development. *The Journal of Jiangsu Administration Institute*. 6(5): 115–121.

Ferraro F., Greenwood R., Loveridge R., Meyer J., Monin P., Sarasvathy S., & Scott D. (2012). Building inclusive markets in rural Bangladesh: How intermediaries work institutional voids. *Academy of Management Journal*. 55(4): 819–850.

Fewsmith J. (2003). The sixteenth national party congress: The succession that didn't happen. *The China Quarterly*. 173(March 2003): 1–16. http://doi.org/10.1017/S0009443903000020

Fidel R. (1984). *The case study method: A case study*. Library & Information Science Research. http://doi.org/10.1108/01409170210782990

Florini A.M., Lai H., & Tan Y. (2012). China Experiments: From local innovations to national reform. *Choice Reviews Online*. 49. The Brookings Institution. http://doi.org/10.5860/CHOICE.49-7127.

Foxon T. J. (2002). Technological and institutional "lock-in" as a barrier to sustainable innovation. *Change*: 1–9. Retrieved from http://www.iccept.ic.ac.uk

Fuguo H. (2012). The relationship between local innovations and economic growth. *Journal of Zhejiang University*. 42(2): 161–177.

Fremeth A. R., & Marcus A. A. (2011). Institutional void and stakeholder leadership: Implementing renewable energy standards in Minnesota. In Burger, J. (ed.). *Stakeholders and scientists*. New York: Springer, pp. 367–392.

Friedrich C. J. (1966). Political pathology. *The Political Quarterly*. 37(1): 70–85.

Fritzen S. A. 2006. Beyond 'political will': how institutional context shapes the implementation of anti-corruption policies. *Policy & Society*. 24(3): 79–96.

Glor E. D. (2001). Key factors influencing innovation in government. *The Innovation Journal: The Public Sector Innovation Journal*. 6(2): 1–19.

Goffin K., & Mitchell R. (2005). *Innovation management: Strategy and implementation using the pentathlon framework*. United Kingdom: Palgrave Macmillan, 359. http://doi.org/10.1108/eb016623

Gong T. (1993). Corruption and reform in China: An analysis of unintended consequences. *Crime, Law and Social Change*. 19: 311–327.

Gong T. (1994). *The Politics of Corruption in Contemporary China: An Analysis of Policy Outcomes*. Westport, CT: Praeger Publishers, USA.

Gong T. (2002). Dangerous collusion: Corruption as a collective venture in contemporary China. *Communist and Post-Communist Studies*. 35(1): 85–103. http://doi.org/10.1016/S0967-067X(01)00026-5

Gong T. (2003). More than mere words, less than hard law: A rhetorical analysis of China's anti-corruption policy. *Public Administration Quarterly*. 27(1/2) (Spring 2003): 159–187.

Gong T. (2006). Corruption and local governance: The double identity of Chinese local governments in market reform. *The Pacific Review*. 19(1): 85–102. http://doi.org/10.1080/09512740500417723

Gong T. (2008). The party discipline inspection in China: Its evolving trajectory and embedded dilemmas. *Crime, Law and Social Change*. 49(2): 139–152. http://doi.org/10.1007/s10611-007-9097-x

Gong T. (2011). An "institutional turn" in integrity management in China. *International Review of Administrative Sciences*. 77(4): 671–686. http://doi.org/10.1177/0020852311419391

Gong T. (2014). Managing government integrity under hierarchy: Anti-corruption efforts in local China. *Journal of Contemporary China*. 24(94): 1–17. http://doi.org/10.1080/10670564.2014.978151

Gong T. (2015). Managing government integrity under hierarchy: Anti-corruption efforts in local China. *Journal of Contemporary China*. 24(94): 684–700.

Gong T., & Ren J. (2013). Hard Rules and soft constraints: Regulating conflict of interest in China. *Journal of Contemporary China*. 22(79): 1–17. http://doi.org/10.1080/10670564.2012.716941

Gong T., & Yang L. (2015). Locally-based integrity management in China: Innovation and significance. *Journal of Guangzhou University* (Social Science Edition). 14: 5–11.

Gong T., & Scott I. (Eds.). (2016). *Routledge handbook of corruption in Asia*. Taylor & Francis.

Guo Y. (2008). Corruption in transitional China: An empirical analysis. *The China Quarterly*. 194(June 2008): 349–364. http://doi.org/10.1017/S0305741008000416

Guo Y. (2012). The evolution of the Chinese communist party discipline inspection commission in the reform era. *China Review*. 1: 1–23.

Gurgur B. T., & Shah A. (2000). Localization and corruption: Panacea or pandora's box? World Bank: 1–37.

Gurgur T., & Shah A. (2002). Localization and corruption: panacea or pandora's box?. In *Managing Fiscal Decentralization* (pp. 62–83). London: Routledge.

Hao Y., & Johnston M. (1995). *China's surge of corruption. Journal of Democracy*. 6(4): 80–94.

Hajer M. (2003). Policy without polity? Policy analysis and the institutional void. *Policy Sciences*. 36(2): 175–195. http://doi.org/10.1023/A:1024834510939

Hargrave T. J., & Van de Ven A. H. (2006). A collective action model of institutional innovation. *Academy of Management Review*. 31(4): 864–888.

He Z. (2000). Corruption and anti-corruption in reform China. *Communist and Post-Communist Studies*. 33(2): 243–270. http://doi.org/10.1016/S0967-067X(00)00006-4

Heywood S. J. (1965). Toward a sound theory of innovation. *The Elementary School Journal*. *66*(3): 107–114.

Heilmann S. (2007). Policy experimentation in China's economic rise. *Studies in Comparative International Development*. 43(1): 1–26. http://doi.org/10.1007/s12116-007-9014-4

Heilmann S. (2008). From local experiments to national policy: the origins of China's distinctive policy process. *The China Journal*, (59), 1–30.

Heilmann S. (2013). From local experiments to national policy: The origins of China's distinctive policy process. *The China Journal*. 59(Jan. 2008): 1–30.

Hodess R., & Wolkers M. (2004). *Report of the transparency international global corruption barometer* 2004. Berlin: TI, https://images.transparencycdn.org/images/2004_GCR_PoliticalCorruption_EN.pdf.

Hodkinson P., & Hodkinson H. (2001). The strengths and limitations of case study research. In learning and skills development agency conference at Cambridge (Vol. 1, No. 1, pp. 5–7). Leeds, UK: University of Leeds.

Hodess R., & Wolkers M. (2004). *Report on the Transparency International Global Corruption Barometer*. Berlin: TI, 9.

Huberts L., Anechiarico F., & Six F. (2008). *Local integrity systems: World cities fighting corruption and safeguarding integrity*. The Hague: BJu Legal Publishers.

Huberts L. W. J. C., & Six F. E. (2012). Local integrity systems. *Public Integrity.* 14(2): 151–172. http://doi.org/10.2753/PIN1099-9922140203

Huntington S. P. (1991). How countries democratize. *Political Science Quarterly.* 106(4): 579–616.

Jin H., Qian Y., & Weingast B. R. (2005). Regional decentralization and fiscal incentives: Federalism, Chinese style. *Journal of Public Economics.* 89(9–10): 1719–1742. http://doi.org/10.1016/j.jpubeco.2004.11.008

Jick T. D. (1979). Mixing qualitative and quantitative methods: Triangulation in action. *Administrative Science Quarterly. 24*(4): 602–611.

Johnston M. (1996). The search for definitions: The vitality of politics and the issue of corruption. *International Social Science Journal. 48*(149): 321–335.

Johnston M. (1999). A brief history of anticorruption agencies. In Schedler, A., Diamond, L. J., & Plattner, M. F. (eds.), *The self-restraining state: Power and accountability in new democracies* (pp. 217–226). Boulder, CO: Lynne Rienner.

Johnston M., & Hao Y. (1995). China's surge in anti-corruption. *Journal of Democracy.* 6(4 (1995): 80–94.

Kanter R. M. (1983). *The change masters: Innovation and productivity in American corporations.* New York: Simon and Schuster.

Kaufman D. (10). Myths about governance and corruption. *Finance and Development, 42*(3), 2005.

Kaufmann D. (1998). Challenges in the Next Stage of Anti-corruption. *New Perspectives on Combating Corruption.* 139–164.

Kay A., & Baker P. (2015). What can causal process tracing offer to policy studies? A review of the literature. *Policy Studies Journal.* 43(1): 1–21. http://doi.org/10.1111/psj.12092

Klijn E. H., & Koppenjan J. F. M. (2006). Institutional design. *Public Management Review.* 8(1): 141–160. http://doi.org/10.1080/14719030500518915

Ko K., & Weng C. (2012). Structural changes in Chinese corruption. *The China Quarterly.* 211(August 2012): 718–740. http://doi.org/10.1017/S0305741012000793

Li C. (2012). The end of the CPC's resilient authoritarianism? A tripartite assessment of shifting power in China. *The China Quarterly.* 211(2012): 595–623. http://doi.org/10.1017/S0305741012000902

Li L. (2001). Support for anti-corruption campaigns in rural China. *Journal of Contemporary China.* 10(29): 573–586.

Li H. (2013). Beyond state-centrism: A historical review of corruption governance in China (In Chinese). *Beijing Cultural Review.* (3): 56–62.

Li H. (2015). Local innovations in reform and integrity building in China: Typological analysis of three cases. *Journal of Beijing University of Aeronautics and Astronautics Social Sciences Edition.* 28(4): 7.

Lu X. (1999). From rank-seeking to rent-seeking: Changing administrative ethos and corruption in reform China. *Crime, Law and Social Change.* 32(4): 347–370. Retrieved from http://www.springerlink.com/index/k4092g38j4t37605.pdf

Lu X. (2000). *Cadres and corruption: The organizational involution of the Chinese Communist Party.* Stanford, CA: Stanford University Press.

Lundvall B. A. (1992). *National systems of innovation: An analytical framework.* London: Pinter.

Luo X. R., & Chung C.-N. (2012). Filling or abusing the institutional void? Ownership and management control of public family businesses in an emerging market. *Organization Science.* 24(2): 591–613. http://doi.org/10.1287/orsc.1120.0751

Manion M. (2004). Lessons for mainland China from anti-corruption reform in Hong Kong. *The China Review*. 4(2): 81–97.
March J. G., & Olsen J. P. (2005). Elaborating the "New Institutionalism" Working Paper No. 11, 1–28.
Marques P. (2011). Theories and policies of innovation: A critical review. *Geography Compass*. 5(11): 838–850. http://doi.org/10.1111/j.1749-8198.2011.00457.x
Meagher P. (2005). Anti-corruption agencies: Rhetoric versus reality. *The Journal of Policy Reform*. 8(1): 69–103. http://doi.org/10.1080/1384128042000328950
Mertha A. C. (2005). China's "soft" centralization: Shifting Tiao/Kuai authority relations. *The China Quarterly*. 184(Dec. 2005): 791–810. http://doi.org/10.1017/S0305741005000500
Michels A., & Van Montfort C. (2013). *The governance of public-private partnerships: Institutional voids in India and China*. Paper prepared for the seminar Institutional Voids during State Re-Scaling, organized by the Erasmus Centre for Emerging Markets in cooperation with the IIAS Centre for Regulation and Governance, on May 13, 2013 in Rotterdam: 1–25.
Mohr L. B. (1969). Determinants of innovation in organizations. *American Political Science Review*. *63*(1): 111–126.
Montes F. J. L., Ruiz Moreno A., & García Morales V. (2005). Influence of support leadership and teamwork cohesion on organizational learning, innovation and performance: An empirical examination. *Technovation*. 25(10): 1159–1172. http://doi.org/10.1016/j.technovation.2004.05.002
Mulvenon J. (2013). *Comrade, Where's My Military Car?* Xi Jinping's throwback mass-line campaign to curb PLA corruption. *China Leadership Monitor*. (42): 1–5.
Nathan A. J. (2003). Authoritarian resilience. *Journal of Democracy*. 14(1): 6–17. http://doi.org/10.1353/jod.2003.0019
Naughton B. (1994). Chinese Institutional innovation and privatization from below. *American Economic Review*. 84(2): 266–270. http://doi.org/10.2307/2117841
Nay O. (2011). What drives reforms in international organizations? External pressure and bureaucratic entrepreneurs in the UN response to AIDS. *Governance*. 24(4): 689–712. http://doi.org/10.1111/j.1468-0491.2011.01545.x
Nelson R. R. (Ed.). (1993). *National innovation systems: A comparative analysis*. Oxford University Press.
Nelson R. R., & Winter S. G. (1977). In search of useful theory of innovation. *Research Policy*. 6(1): 36–76. http://doi.org/10.1016/0048-7333(77)90029-4
Ngo T. W. (2009). Governing Rapid Growth in Asia: State-led Development in Historical Perspective. Address given at the occasion of accepting the appointment as Extraordinary Professor of History of Asia at the Faculty of History and Arts Erasmus University Rotterdam on 16 October 2009.
Ngo T. (2015). Social movements under institutional voids: The success and failure of the anti-corruption movement in Taiwan. *Asian Studies*. 1(1): 99–120. http://doi.org/10.6551/AS.0101.05
Ni X., & Huang H. (2013). Intellectual consensus, top-level design and institutional turning of anti-corruption activities (in Chinese). *Theoretical Horizon*. (3): 44–47.
Ni, X., & Sun. Z. F. (2015). Factor analysis of public perception on anti-corruption efforts: Evidence from 21 municipal cities of Guangdong province (2003–2012). *Political Studies* (in Chinese): 71–85.
Nye J. S. (1967). Corruption and political development: A cost-benefit analysis. *American Political Science Review*. 61(2): 417–427.

Ojha N. P., Ghosh P., Khandelwal S., & Kapoor H. (2011). Innovation overview. *Business Today*, 53–56.

Pei M. (2006). The dark side of China's rise. *Foreign Policy*, (153), 32.

Persson A., Rothstein B., & Teorell J. (2013). Why anti-corruption reforms fail: Systemic corruption as a collective action problem. *Governance*. 26(3): 449–471. http://doi.org/10.1111/j.1468-0491.2012.01604.x

Pope J., & Vogl F. (2000). Making anticorruption agencies more effective. *Finance and Development*. *37*(2): 6.

Post L. A., Raile A. N., & Raile E. D. (2010). Defining political will. *Politics & Policy*. 38(4): 653–676.

Qin Y. (2013). *Financial resources for anti-corruption in contemporary China: Determinants and consequences of regional diversity*. Chinese University of Hong Kong.

Quade E. A. (2007). The logic of anti-corruption enforcement campaigns in contemporary China. *Journal of Contemporary China*. 16(50): 65–77. http://doi.org/10.1080/10670560601026751

Quah J. S. (1999). Corruption in Asian countries: Can it be minimized?. *Public Administration Review*. (Vol. 2: pp. 483–494).

Quah J. S. T. (2006). Curbing Asian corruption: An impossible dream? *Current History*. 105(690): 176–179.

Raffaelli, R., & Glynn, M. A. (2015). Institutional innovation: Novel, useful. In: *The Oxford handbook of creativity, innovation, and entrepreneurship*, 407–420.

Ren J. (2010). The critical points in reforming the anti-corruption system in China in the future: Anti-corruption agencies and system. *Theory Reference*, 1

Remneland-Wikhamn B., Ljungberg J. A. N., Bergquist M., & Kuschel J. (2011). Open innovation, generativity and the supplier as peer: The case of iPhone and android. *International Journal of Innovation Management*. *15*(01): 205–230.

Rogers E. M., & Shoemaker F. (1971). *Communication of innovation: A cross-cultural approach*. New York: Free Press.

Rothstein B. (2007). *Anti-corruption: A big-bang theory* (February 6, 2009). QoG Working Paper No. 2007:3. Available at SSRN: https://ssrn.com/abstract=1338614 or http://dx.doi.org/10.2139/ssrn.1338614

Rothstein B. (2011). Anti-corruption: The indirect 'big bang' approach. *Review of International Political Economy*. 18(2): 228–250. http://doi.org/10.1080/09692291003607834

Schmieding H. (1991). *From socialism to an institutional void: Notes on the nature of the transformation crisis* (No. 480). Kiel Working Paper.

Shah A. (2006). WPS3824 *Corruption and Decentralized Public Governance*. Policy Research Working Paper; No. 3824. World Bank, Washington, DC. © World Bank. https://openknowledge.worldbank.org/handle/10986/8805

Shambaugh D. (2008). *China's communist party: Atrophy and adaptation*. Berkeley: University of California Press.

Shirk S. (2007). *China: Fragile superpower*. New York: Oxford University Press.

Sørensen E., & Waldorff S. B. (2014). Collaborative policy innovation: Problems and potential. *The Innovation Journal: The Public Sector Innovation Journal*. 19(3): 1–17.

Stephan U., Uhlaner L. M., & Stride C. (2015). Institutions and social entrepreneurship: The role of institutional voids, institutional support, and institutional configurations. *Journal of International Business Studies*. 46(3): 308–331. http://doi.org/10.1057/jibs.2014.38

Sun Y. (2004). *Corruption and market in contemporary China*. New York: Cornell University Press.

Sun Y. (2005). Corruption, growth, and reform: The Chinese enigma. *Current History*. 104(683): 257–263.

Tanzi V. (1998). *Corruption around the world*. IMF Staff Papers, 45(4): 559–594.

Themudo, N. S. (2013). Reassessing the impact of civil society: nonprofit sector, press freedom, and corruption. *Governance*. 26(1): 63–89.

Thompson V. A. (1965). Bureaucracy and innovation. *Administrative Science Quarterly*, 1–20.

Tsai K. S. (2006). *Changing China: Private entrepreneurs and adaptive informal institutions*. Paper prepared for the conference "Capitalism with Chinese Characteristics: China's Political Economy in Comparative and Theoretical Perspective." Indiana University, May 19–20, 2006.

Tsai W.-H., & Dean N. (2014). Experimentation under hierarchy in local conditions: Cases of political reform in Guangdong and Sichuan, China. *The China Quarterly*. 218: 339–358. http://doi.org/10.1017/S0305741014000630

United Nations Development Programme. (2005). *Institutional arrangements to combat corruption: A comparative study*.

Van de Ven A. H. (1986). Central Problems in the management of innovation. *Management Science*. 32(5): 590–607. http://doi.org/10.2307/2631848

Walker R. M. (2006). Innovation type and diffusion: An empirical analysis of local government. *Public Administration*. 84(2): 311–335.

Wang C.Y. (2009). Anti-corruption innovation of local governments since the reform and opening up in China (in Chinese). *New Horizons*. (4): 48–50.

Wedeman, A. (2002). *Cadres and corruption: The organizational involution of the Chinese Communist Party*. By Xiaobo Lu. Stanford: Stanford University Press, 2000.

WedemanA.(2004).TheintensificationofcorruptioninChina.*JournalofContemporary China*. 35(116): 85–103. http://dx.doi.org/10.1080/1067056042000300808

Wedeman A. (2005). Anti-corruption campaigns and the intensification of corruption in China. *Journal of Contemporary China*. 14(42): 93–116. http://doi.org/10.1080/1067056042000300808

Wolfe R. A. (1994). Organizational innovation: Review, critique and suggested research directions. *Journal of Management Studies*. 31(3): 405–431.

Woodhill J. (2010). Capacities for institutional innovation: A complexity perspective. *IDS Bulletin*. 41(3): 47–59. http://doi.org/10.1111/j.1759-5436.2010.00136.x

Wu Y., & Zhu J. (2011). Corruption, anti-corruption, and inter-county income disparity in China. *The Social Science Journal*. 48(3): 435–448. http://doi.org/10.1016/j.soscij.2011.05.001

Wu, J., Ma, L., & Yang, Y. (2013). Innovation in the Chinese public sector: Typology and distribution. *Public Administration*. 91(2): 347–365.

Xuedong C., & Xuelian Y. (2009). Promoting local government innovations, local cadres' view. *Journal of Public Management*. 1–22.

Yang D. L. (2006). Economic transformation and its political discontents in China: Authoritarianism, unequal growth, and the dilemmas of political development. *Annual Review of Political Science*. 9(1): 143–164. http://doi.org/10.1146/annurev.polisci.9.062404.170624

Yang, X. (2013). *Local Government Reform in China in the Past Ten Years: an Evaluation Based on the Chinese Local Governance Innovations Awards*. CDDRL Working Papers. Stanford University, Stanford, CA.

Yep R. (2015). Filling the institutional void in rural land markets in Southern China: Is there room for spontaneous change from below? *Development and Change*. 46(3): 534–561. http://doi.org/10.1111/dech.12161

Yin R. K. (2008). *Case study research: Design and methods* (Third Ed., Vol. 5). SAGE Publications.

Yong G. (2007). *Economic transition, institution and corruption*. Beijing: Social Science Academic Press (China).

Yu Q. (2013). Financial resources for anti-corruption in contemporary China: determinants and consequences of regional diversity. Ph.D. Thesis. Chinese University of Hong Kong.

Zhan, J. V. (2011). Natural resources and corruption: Empirical evidence from China. In Annual Meeting of American Political Science Association.

Zhao Q. (2012). The regional disparities in Chinese provincial government innovation. *Innovation: Management, Policy and Practice*. 14(4): 595–604.

Zhou, L. A. (2007). Governing China's local officials: An analysis of promotion tournament model. *Economic Research Journal*. *7*(36): 36–50.

Zhou X. (2009). The institutional logic of collusion among local governments in China. *Modern China*. 36(1): 47–78. http://doi.org/10.1177/0097700409347970

Zhu J. (2008). *The institutional determinants of anti-corruption in China: Evidences from revealed corruption cases across provinces*. Paper presented at the annual meeting of the MPSA Annual National Conference, Palmer House Hotel, Hilton, Chicago, IL. Online. http://citation.allacademic.com/meta/p268087_index.html

Zhu X. (2014). Difficulty in promoting the innovation experience of local government—*Review of the Research on the Public Policy Innovation Diffusion Theory*. 63–77.

Zhu X. (2014). Mandate versus championship: Vertical government intervention and diffusion of innovation in public services in authoritarian China. *Public Management Review*. 16(1): 117–139. http://doi.org/10.1080/14719037.2013.798028

Zhu J., & Zhang G. (2008). The institutional determinants of anticorruption in China: Evidences from revealed corruption cases across provinces. In *paper, Midwest Political Science Association annual conference, Chicago*.

Zhuang D. (2014). A reflection on the central government's anti-corruption strategy. *New Report*. 2: 22–23.

Index

Italicized and **bold** pages refer to figures and tables respectively, and page numbers followed by "n" refer to notes.